TROLLEYBUS MEMORIES
WOLVERHAMPTON

Eric T. Challoner

First published 2007

ISBN (10) 0 7110 3214 9
ISBN (13) 978 0 7110 3214 9

© Eric T. Challoner 2007

Published by Ian Allan Publishing

an imprint of Ian Allan Publishing Ltd, Hersham, Surrey, KT12 4RG
Printed in England by Ian Allan Printing Ltd, Hersham, Surrey, KT12 4RG

Code: 0702/B

Visit the Ian Allan Publishing website at www.ianallanpublishing.com

Front cover, upper: Wolverhampton's last female trolleybus driver, Amy Davies, brings Sunbeam F4 626 round the corner into Garrick Street past the Savoy cinema, at the start of a trip to Dudley.

Front cover, lower: Roe-bodied Sunbeam W4 sisters 442 and 441 at Oxford Street, Bilston, in June 1964, on their way to Darlaston and Great Bridge Road. Fraser Street reverser can be seen behind 441.

Back cover: On the last Saturday of operation, 4 March 1967, Sunbeam/Roe trolleys, including 432 and 435, are seen working the ever-busy section at Fighting Cocks, their drivers determined to go out in style.

Title page: Having reversed into Downham Place, Sunbeam 453 will draw forward off the reverser, turning right into Jeffcock Road and around the corner to stop at the Rayleigh Road loading point. *John Hughes collection*

*For Lucky
1984 – 2003
My feline friend
and companion
down all the days*

Contents

Foreword

Standing some 650ft above sea level on a bed of red sandstone, Wolverhampton lies 120 miles north of London, on the edge of the Black Country between Stafford and Birmingham, with the border county of Shropshire on its western flank. City status was granted on 18 December 2000, but for the purpose of this history all text refers to the 'town', as, indeed, it was in the days of trolleybus operation; likewise all reference to money is shown, where appropriate, in the pre-decimal style of pounds, shillings and pence, to reflect the coinage in use at that time.

The author, who was born in New Street, Wednesfield, within yards of the original tram terminus, has had a fascination for trolleybuses for as long as he can remember and started collecting information back in the early 1960s. Drawing heavily on personal observations and recorded notes, the result is this book, a true labour of love. There are still many unresolved areas. Where was the Heath Town turning-point? Did trolleybuses enter the early Tettenhall reverser or back in and drive out, and what was the purpose of the East–North spur at the junction of Bushbury Road and Thorneycroft Lane? The answers to these and other questions are still to be uncovered. One day they may be resolved. Until then, sit back and enjoy the read!

Acknowledgements

Although every effort has been made to ensure accuracy, the passage of time, coupled with fading memories and conflicting dates in a number of other sources, has resulted in one or two grey areas, with some details open to question. The author would be pleased to accept any new information. Whilst all photographs have been credited where known, it has not been possible to trace or contact all copyright owners.

I am indebted to the following and would like to place on record my thanks to them (in no particular order) for their enthusiastic encouragement and patience in answering a multitude of enquiries during the preparation of this book: John Hughes, Deryk N. Vernon, Fred G. Richardson, David E. Smith and John Benton. I hope the result will prove to be both an informative and entertaining history of the trolleybus in Wolverhampton.

Eric T. Challoner
Wellington
January 2007

Introduction

Wolverhampton was first established as a settlement in 985 AD, at which time Æthelred II 'The Unready' (979-1013, 1014-1016) occupied the English throne. The younger son of Edgar, he became king at the age of seven, following the murder of his half-brother Edward II in 978 at Corfe Castle by Edward's own supporters. In 985 King Æthelred granted lands in the area to his sister, Lady Wulfrun. These lay in the small settlement known as Heantun. In 994 Lady Wulfrun endowed a monastery and church there. The settlement subsequently became known as Hampton, and in time the prefix 'Wulfrun' was added to avoid confusion with similarly named places nearby, the name eventually devolving to Wolverhampton. A new church was built c1190 and re-dedicated to St Peter in 1258, during which time a charter was granted by Henry II to hold a market in the town (which practice has continued on a weekly basis ever since), the ensuing wool trade continuing to prosper until the middle of the 16th century, when it declined with the growth of woollen cloth production in Yorkshire. The town became involved in the development of numerous different trades, and by the middle of the 19th century Wolverhampton had become a centre for ironmongery, lock-making and the manufacture of tinplate.

By 1730 the town had a population of over 7,000. There is documented evidence for what was probably a very basic stagecoach service three times a week between Wolverhampton and Birmingham. The first daily horse-drawn coach, linking the town to neighbouring Walsall, began operating in July 1783. Further services followed and by 1818 connected Wolverhampton with destinations as far away as Manchester, Bristol and London. However, by the early 1830s long-distance services were declining in the face of expanding railway competition, leaving only local services, themselves under increasing threat from private horse buses. Records show that George Bayley started the first recorded omnibus service in 1833, using a nine-seat coach. In 1835 he was followed by John Doughty, who operated a service to Birmingham, being joined on this route in 1836 by the Midlands Omnibus Co and the Birmingham Omnibus Conveyance Co. Following the introduction of horse trams, horse-drawn omnibus services soon faded from the scene, being unable to compete financially.

The origins of electric transport in Wolverhampton can be traced back to 22 September 1876, when a letter to the Town Clerk from a Mr Webb in London led to a meeting with a group of influential gentlemen, resulting in the incorporation on 14 December that year of the privately owned Wolverhampton Tramways Co. Lines set to a standard gauge of 4ft 8$\frac{1}{2}$in between the rails were laid between Queen Square, in the centre of town, and Newbridge, to the west. The first horse-drawn service left Queen Square at 8am on 1 May 1878 for the 12-minute journey to Newbridge, a fare of 2d being charged. Further routes were introduced, and some experimentation with steam trams was attempted, though the Council refused to grant permission for these to continue beyond October 1881. The Wolverhampton Tramways Act was passed in 1899, purchase of all tramways within the borough becoming effective from 1 May 1900, the BET group retaining control of those beyond.

On 6 February 1902, following conversion of a horse-tram route to a new track gauge of 3ft 6in, the first electric tram service was inaugurated, from Cleveland Road to Ettingshall Road. From the very start the Corporation was to follow a different pattern from other towns and for its trams invested heavily in the untried and largely unknown Lorain system of surface contact, whereby rectangular metal studs, set between the rails at regular intervals, made contact with a centrally located 12ft-long phosphor-bronze metal skate underneath the tram as it passed along. The electrically connected studs were magnetically activated by the passage of the skate, thus drawing power for the tram's motor. (The National Tramway Museum has an example of the stud on display.)

The Council's decision to use the Lorain system rather than draw power from more conventional overhead wires was heavily influenced by the Council Chairman, Alderman Mander, who was adamantly opposed to any form of 'unsightly' wiring disfiguring the town's streets. There was also a darker reason behind this posture, as the good burghers of Wolverhampton did not want the BET-group trams, operating widely across the Black Country, to gain a foothold in the town and thus draw revenue away from the Council, although they were to enter the town for a brief period between 1906 and 1909 using cars specially fitted with dual collection equipment.

Over time a network of eight routes, including converted horse-tram lines, was subsequently equipped for Lorain operation and ran with varying degrees of success until 1919. In October of that year the General Manager, Charles Owen Silvers, submitted to the Tramways Committee a report emphasising the state of the by then badly worn track and the urgent need for renewal. The isolationist policy of the last 17 years was making itself felt, replacement parts being now unobtainable.

The conclusion drawn was that conversion to an overhead system of supply was not only inevitable but was now required on an urgent basis. It fell to Sir Charles Mander (created a Baronet by King George V in 1911) to present the proposal to Council, the cost of conversion being £375,000; this cannot have sat easily with Sir Charles in view of his violent opposition to the idea back in 1901. The programme was carried out under the personal direction of the General Manager, and erection of overhead line traction poles commenced on 26 January 1921, the first trams running on the Dudley road by 26 March and complete conversion of the system being achieved by 19 October. This situation would not last, however, as the years had taken their toll on equipment. Lack of maintenance during World War 1 had also left the system with badly worn track in several areas. This, coupled with an obsolete method of current collection that was constantly being shored up by Transport Department employees (the Lorain studs failing on an almost daily basis), meant that a decision had to be taken urgently on the direction that the Corporation would now take regarding public transport in Wolverhampton, and thus the way was paved for the introduction of the trolleybus.

In retrospect it can be said that adoption of the Lorain system, with no proven track record, was a brave but foolhardy attempt by a council seemingly dogged by internal politics and with a 'not in my backyard' attitude to overhead electrification. Despite the proven benefits the councillors were utterly determined to plough their own furrow, and that they were led (and in some cases coerced) by one particular Alderman intent on dominating the proceedings cannot be denied. The result was a venture that was inevitably doomed to failure. As for the secondary reason for staying with the system — keeping BET and its associated companies out of Wolverhampton for many years, to the financial benefit of the Council — it is difficult to assess just how much was lost to the townspeople in the way of commercial development and investment.

1. The Coming of The Trolleybus

A visit to Birmingham on 16 January 1923 was organised by the Transport Committee with a view to inspecting the trolleybus system that Birmingham Corporation had installed on 27 November 1922 to replace the ageing tramcar service to the Nechells district. Having assessed its suitability for Wolverhampton's streets the Committee came away comfortable in the knowledge that it would be recommending a satisfactory alternative to the tramway system then in use.

The General Manager, Charles Owen Silvers, presented a report recommending that, rather than reconstructing the tramway track on the Wednesfield route and re-laying the single line as double track, this should be converted to trolleybus operation and trialled for its suitability for Wolverhampton's streets. In March

the Council approved the Committee's recommendation, though the need for additional wiring was not specifically discussed or considered. The move to trolleybus was to make Wolverhampton a leader in the field of conversion; second only to Birmingham, it became the 14th trolleybus operator and only the third to convert from trams.

Trams ceased running on the 1³/₄-mile route from Broad Street to New Street on 23 July 1923, a motor-bus service being substituted for the duration of the conversion. The new service commenced on 29 October. The route ran 2¹/₄ miles to a turning-circle in the entrance to Neachells Lane, by the Dog & Partridge public house and just short of Pinfold Bridge, being a short way beyond the original tram terminus. To begin the service six new vehicles were pur-

chased from Tilling-Stevens. Numbered 1-6, these were TS6 models fitted with Dodson centre-entrance 40-seat bodies (re-seated to 36 in November 1927) on converted petrol-electric chassis, with the engine and generator removed and electrical traction gear installed. Until additional wiring was erected the trolleybuses could reach Cleveland Road depot only by using one trolley boom on the overhead wire and trailing a metal skate on the tram rail to provide an earth return for the current.

The service was trialled for one year. Although the Corporation possessed no statutory powers to operate trolleybuses, the Minister of Transport confirmed that, if the local authorities affected had no objections, he would not stand in the way.

With the operation proving to be a complete success, the decision was taken

Above: Wolverhampton's first trolleybus, a Tilling-Stevens TS6, on a run prior to the official opening on Monday 29 October 1923. It has been specially posed on the corner of New Street, at the old tram terminus, facing towards Wolverhampton. Rookery Canal Bridge can be seen in the background. The canal bridge is still there, but this end of New Street has been lost to redevelopment of the area, with a public house fronting the main road at this point. *John Hughes collection*

to replace all remaining trams with trolleybuses. The line to Bushbury was in dire need of conversion, as the track was badly worn. The tram route left town via Darlington Street and Waterloo Road, but a decision was taken to route the new trolleybus service out by Wulfruna Street and in by North Street and Queen Square. On 19 August 1924 the trams were replaced with a substitute bus service using hired vehicles. Between 24 January and 14 March 1925 seven more Tilling-Stevens vehicles arrived to supplement the trolleybus fleet. Trolleybuses commenced running on 9 March 1925, with the opportunity being taken to extend the route beyond the original tram terminus along Stafford Road to the Vine Inn at Fordhouses, although at that time there were few houses in the vicinity. On the same date a short-working loop was installed at the Greenwood Road turn (from 1927 adjacent to the Goodyear tyre factory). A further turning-circle was constructed at the junction of Stafford Road and Bushbury Lane, where the tram route ended, and extra journeys were operated to this point from 23 April. In time, as housing development progressed further into the countryside, the turning-circle would be lifted.

For the 1924/5 football season traffic at the Molineux ground was still handled by trams, using the special siding at the north end of Waterloo Road, but after 1925 trolleybuses and motor buses dealt with this. This left tram routes to Tettenhall, Willenhall, Whitmore Reans, Bilston, Lea Road and Fighting Cocks, where route 8 met the Wolverhampton District Electric Tramway Co line from Dudley.

During 1924 the Transport Committee had undertaken negotiations with BET regarding the operation of trolleybuses on the Dudley route. However, this was complicated by the fact that various sections beyond Fighting Cocks were owned by more than one local authority and in one part leased back to WDET. After a great deal of negotiation agreement was reached in principle. It had been intended to transfer ownership on 1 January 1925, but delays in obtaining the necessary powers left WDET continuing to operate the service whilst receiving a monthly payment from the Corporation. Royal Assent was given on 7 August for the Wolverhampton Corporation Act 1925, confirming agreement for the purchase of the Fighting Cocks–Dudley section of tramway and granting the Corporation powers to operate trolleybuses through to Dudley. At midnight on 14/15 August the Corporation took over the routes and depot at Sedgley, together with 66 of WDET's employees. Eight Corporation cars were transferred to the depot, and six Company cars borrowed on a temporary basis.

The changeover operation now gathered pace. The line to Fighting Cocks succumbed on 18 August 1925, seven further trolleys being due to arrive in October to operate the new service.

On 25 October trams ceased running between Fighting Cocks and Sedgley, this made possible by the acquisition on 15 August of the Fighting Cocks–Dudley section of tramway from WDET. The replacement Sedgley trolley, numbered 8A, did not start running until all wiring had been completed, on 10 November 1926; overhead linemen having installed trolley wires as far as Sedgley tram depot, the Sedgley–Eve Hill section and tram depot had ceased operation on 7 November. The countryside along this stretch was quite moor-like, being at a height of 700ft and on a natural ridge or plateau rich in Silurian limestone, from which many of the local walls were constructed, with rough grassland dropping gently down to the east to the valley of the Tame, where the chimney stacks of the 'black country' rose into the sky like a primordial metal forest. West of the road the land fell steeply down an escarpment, the Stour Valley below revealing a more pastoral scene that cradled the villages of Wombourne and Himley, both served by the Great Western Railway branch from Tettenhall.

In all cases of conversion the intervening time between tram and trolleybus was covered by a substitute motor-bus service. The full sequence of conversion was as follows:

Section of route covered	Trams withdrawn	Trolleybuses introduced
Snow Hill–Fighting Cocks	18/08/25	26/10/25
Fighting Cocks–Sedgley (Junction Inn)	25/10/25	10/11/26 (to Bull Ring)
Junction Inn–Eve Hill	07/11/26	11/05/27 (to Sedgley depot)
Eve Hill–Dudley	c08/26	08/07/27 (to Dudley, Stone Street)

Since its inception the Bushbury–Fordhouses route had, from the Town Hall starting point in North Street, travelled via Queen Square, Lichfield Street and Wulfruna Street in an anti-clockwise direction around St Peter's Collegiate Church and through the northern half of Princes Square. This changed on 22 December 1925, with trolleys running direct via Wulfruna Street, the traffic island at its junction with Stafford Street being provided with a turning-circle, thus completing a full circle of wiring with the Wednesfield service already using the island to return down Broad Street.

The General Strike of 1926 was to affect the transport services across the country. It commenced on 3 May, and at first there was a complete stoppage across most of the country, but gradually over the ensuing days some semblance of order returned. In Wolverhampton there was initially a total cessation, but by 11 May a motor-bus service of sorts, manned by volunteers, was being run by the staff of Guy Motors Ltd.

The Wolverhampton Corporation Bill 1925 had sought to establish a through service of trolleybuses between Wolverhampton and Walsall. The Bill was heard concurrently with another promoted by Walsall Corporation, which was seeking powers to operate trolleybuses to Willenhall and, by means of a joint-working agreement, to establish a through service between the two towns. Powers were eventually secured to convert the required lines, although Bilston Urban District Council's rooted opposition successfully blocked conversion of a local tram line. Powers were also obtained for construction of trolleybus routes to Springhill, Penn and Aldersley, via Hordern Road. Track on the Willenhall Road was in urgent need of renewal, and following a negotiated agreement the Corporation purchased the section between Deans Road and Market Place, Willenhall, from Wolverhampton District Tramways Ltd, for £6,263. The agreement allowed possession from 9 August 1926, when the Corporation began running a substitute motor-bus service, the trams having given up occupation the previous night.

The ongoing tram-to-trolleybus conversion programme had been broadly in line with the General Manager's report to the Transport Committee (a title assumed in February 1926), presented to the Council in June 1926. In his report the General Manager had advised that large-scale expenditure would be required to renew the Penn Fields, Tettenhall and Willenhall routes, citing the worn-out state of the tram tracks. After some debate it was agreed that in the fullness of time these routes would be converted to trolleybus operation, but the Whitmore Reans route was marked down for motor buses.

Seven more new Tilling-Stevens trolleybuses were destined to enter service during 1926. On 1 December the Corporation took delivery of the first trolleybus to come from Guy Motors, a company in business since 1914 and noted for its flair and innovation, with a wide range of vehicles to its credit. The trolley consisted of a BTX chassis with Dodson bodywork and was the first to be fitted with pneumatic tyres, being the only trolleybus in the fleet to have an open staircase. As with all Guy trolleybuses of this period, regenerative braking was fitted, in this instance using a compound-wound motor incorporating Rees-Stevens-type regenerative control.

Numbered 33, it entered service on the Sedgley route. Fifteen more of these vehicles were to arrive in 1927, and a further eight in 1928.

On 16 May 1927, using single-deck vehicles, trolleybus services commenced on the Willenhall route from the new starting-point in Horseley Fields as far as Neachells Lane, this being extended on 16 September to Willenhall town centre, where a turning-circle was erected at the market place. (Eventually this circle would be used by Walsall Corporation for its short workings and as a terminus for the yet-to-be initiated trolleybus service from Bilston and Fighting Cocks.) In December Walsall Corporation did a political about-turn, now declaring that it no longer regarded the trolleybus as an economic proposition, despite a declared intention to the contrary in the Bill promoted in 1925. Wolverhampton Corporation stated that it could not accept this stance, and after much hard negotiating it was agreed that, if receipts on this route reached a required minimum, Walsall would convert to trolleybus.

The Penn Fields section was next in line for conversion, the last tram making its way back to town on the night of Sunday 20 March 1927; the following day saw a motor-bus service commence between Victoria Square and Duke Street in Penn Fields, and by Sunday 27 March 85 men were at work removing track from Queen Square and Victoria Street. A batch of double-deck trolleybuses relaunched the service on 11 July, a turning-circle having been

erected at the junction of Lea Road and Stubbs Road, some 300yd short of the old tram terminus at the top of what had been previously known as Stubbs Lane.

On 10 July the Tettenhall route lost its trams. Despite the fact that this was the route on which, 49 years earlier, horse trams had inaugurated the tram service the Corporation chose not to mark the occasion, displaying a trait that was to become all too familiar in later years. After the usual period of motor-bus cover a partial service was instituted to Wergs Road on 29 November, a full service, terminating in Wrottesley Road, starting on 2 January 1928. The new terminus was in a very narrow section of road, and the reversing-triangle here was soon replaced by the more familiar turning-circle outside the Dog & Gun public house. The commencement of the service and the journey of the first trolleybus down the route were reported in depth by the town's press, records stating that the event was well received locally, with many people queuing to purchase the 3d ticket and travel through what was still considered the elite area of town to Tettenhall terminus.

The removal of trams from the Whitmore Reans service came hard on the heels of the Tettenhall closure, with the service ceasing on 1 October 1927. A motor-bus service to Crowther Road commenced operation the following day, this being extended on 15 October 1928 to form a circular service into the Whitmore Reans estate, route 2 running clockwise via Court Road and the 2A anti-clockwise via

Hunter Street and Hordern Road. Trolleybuses now operated to Tettenhall, Fordhouses, Penn Fields, Willenhall, Wednesfield and Dudley, leaving just the Bilston area still covered by trams.

Wolverhampton was to play host to the first set of electrically operated traffic lights in Britain. Located in Princes Square, these were connected experimentally on Saturday 5 November 1927, and, following satisfactory trials, made permanent in October 1928. A single existing traction pole in the centre of the square was provided with three-aspect lamps hung to face each of the four exits, and below each set was hung the famous blue enamelled sign bearing the legend 'TURNING RIGHT — KEEP RIGHT'. This became well known to trolleybus drivers turning out of Stafford Street and Broad Street into Lichfield Street on their way out of town.

Since 1925 an agreement had been sought with BET for the purchase of all remaining tram lines in the Bilston area. This was concluded on 9 October 1926 but did not receive Royal Assent until 3 August 1928. The Corporation took over some of the WDET lines on 27 August, the remainder and Bilston depot coming under its control on 1 September. The Corporation-owned tram services had finished on the night of 26 August with car 56, under the control of Conductor E. Paddock, making a last run, through driving rain, from Bilston to Wolverhampton. The irony was that just five days later, on 1 September, the Corporation was to become a tramway

Above: **A general view of the overhead wiring within the Courtaulds factory.** *John Hughes collection*

Above: Prior to delivery Guy BTX 59, in full Wolverhampton livery, saw brief loan in Nottingham, to determine the suitability or otherwise of using six-wheel trolleybuses in that city. It is seen here at the junction of King Street and Queen Street on the Mansfield Road route. *John Hughes collection*

owner again when it took over the local Bilston services. Included in the takeover were 15 trams based at Bilston depot, the depot itself (a Grade II-listed building originally opened in 1900) along with the depot house next door at 34 Mount Pleasant, plus 61 staff, including 18 pairs of drivers and conductors. This was supplemented by at least two double-deck Corporation cars, which worked the Willenhall–Darlaston service via Bilston, perpetuating the WDET policy of running this route as a through service.

Tramway operation was to continue for only a short period before each route succumbed to motor-bus operation pending the introduction of trolleybuses. Bilston–Fighting Cocks finished on 25 November, and the remaining routes, including Willenhall–Darlaston, ceased on 30 November. This date saw the closure to trams of both Bilston and Sedgley depots, marking the very end of tramway operation by Wolverhampton Corporation. Following conversion the various sections were reopened for trolleybus working as follows:

The Darlaston section was opened using trolleybus No 60, a Guy BTX with Dodson bodywork, which worked the first journey from the Bull Stake at Darlaston. Unusually, the destination route box displayed the number 1 for the occasion! For trolleys coming from Bilston a turning-circle at Fighting Cocks, at the junction of Parkfield Road and Dudley Road, was used initially, although its use declined after 8 October 1934, when services on route 8 were extended a short distance further down Wolverhampton Road East towards Dudley, a new turning-circle having been provided at the entrance to Dudding Road, to be shared with services 8A and 8B, incoming movements on Sedgley and Dudley workings being facilitated by use of a new passing-loop in the new overhead layout. The Corporation was not yet satisfied, and early in May 1930 the reversing-triangle in Walsall Street was lifted and reinstalled in

Fraser Street, nearer Bilston town centre. This was to see frequent use by timetabled journeys on route 7 until October 1949, as well as intermittent workings plus daily depot movements thereafter, and a smooth and safe reversal into the awkward opening of Fraser Street, next to the tree-lined Methodist churchyard, required the undivided attention of the conductor.

Constituting an unusual addition to the network were the wires that led into the Courtaulds factory, an American-owned facility set up in 1916 to produce viscose yarn and eventually employing more than 3,500 workers. Opened at the same time as the Whitmore Reans section and reached via the wiring for route 2A, the branch turned right off Hordern Road and through the main entrance, running thereafter for some 360yd to a turning-loop. The extension had been authorised at the September 1929 meeting of the Transport Committee and was considered sufficiently important by Courtaulds for the company to pay the erection costs of £450. Special trolleybus services were provided for factory workers and ran to Low Hill, the town centre and Merry Hill.

Wolverhampton–Bilston	19/11/28
Bilston–Darlaston	27/05/29 (as a through route from Wolverhampton)
Wolverhampton–Whitmore Reans	27/01/30 (now part of a through service to Darlaston)
Fighting Cocks–Bilston–Willenhall	27/10/30 (as a through route)

The ex-WDET tram depots at Bilston and Sedgley were surplus to requirements at the time of takeover, but, with expansion in mind, Wolverhampton Corporation had retained both for eventual use with trolleybuses. The depot house, also a Grade II-listed building, had originally been occupied by the manager of WDET and in later years was to become the home of Howard Davies, Chief Motor Traffic Inspector for Wolverhampton Corporation.

Being on quite narrow sites, both depots were equipped with turntables, the turntable and pit at Bilston costing £565. Turntables on trolleybus systems were something of a rarity in the UK, there being only four; the other two were at Christchurch, on the Bournemouth system, and at the hilly and somewhat windswept Longwood terminus in Huddersfield. In later years the 'table at Bilston proved to be notoriously stiff and required several pairs of hands to turn a vehicle.

While conversion was effected the motor buses used on the Fighting Cocks–Willenhall section were outstationed at Bilston depot, crews being ferried out on a daily basis from Cleveland Road by special bus, thereby releasing the former tram drivers to be retrained for trolleybus work. The depot reopened for trolleybus operation on 27 October 1930 and was eventually able to accommodate 25 vehicles.

Sedgley depot had been occupied by the 'Midland Red' buses of the Birmingham & Midland Motor Omnibus Co from 13 December 1919, when that firm started operating a motor bus to Bilston and on to the Wolverhampton boundary at Ettingshall, but by 14 May 1920 these had moved to premises in Bilston Street, Wolverhampton. Following its conversion from a tram depot Sedgley began operation with trolleybuses on 10 February 1930, housing vehicles for routes 8, 8A and 8B; it finally closed on 31 October 1938.

One Wolverhampton trolleybus was to see brief service elsewhere as an ambassador, this being No 59, a Guy BTX with Dodson bodywork. A three-axle vehicle, it was loaned to Nottingham, in full Wolverhampton livery and probably just prior to its official delivery to Wolverhampton, in 1929. At that time Nottingham had opened one trolleybus route from the city centre to Basford, using two-axle double-deck trolleybuses, and wanted to assess the suitability of a three-axle vehicle for its ongoing tramway-conversion programme. The test having proved satisfactory, three-axle vehicles were subsequently obtained, although this did not result in any orders for Guy Motors.

During 1928 route numbers were allocated to both trolleybus and motor-bus routes, and the entire fleet was fitted with service-number boxes. These showed numbers only at the front and rear, the destination being displayed in the middle windows of the lower saloon. The first allocation used several A- and B- suffixed numbers. From 1931 roller blinds were fitted to the front, side and rear of vehicles, showing the route number and outer destination on one blind. Inward-bound vehicles showed 'Wolverhampton' only, with no route number displayed. Route numbers were to alter on occasion, as various cross-town services were amended and combined. Trolleybus routes (and intended conversions) as at 1929 were as follows:

1	Tettenhall	6	Heath Town	9B	Low Hill #.
2	Whitmore Reans (via Court Road) *	6A	Wednesfield	11	Mount Road #
2A	Whitmore Reans (via Hordern Road) *	7	Bilston *	11A	Penn #
		7A	Darlaston *	12	Finchfield (via Bradmore) #
3	Bushbury	8	Fighting Cocks		
3A	Fordhouses	8A	Sedgley	13	Merry Hill ##
4	Penn Fields	8B	Dudley	24	Willenhall–Bilston +
5	Willenhall	9	Amos Lane #	25	Willenhall–Fighting Cocks +
5A	Walsall **	9A	Bushbury Hill ##		

* These motor-bus routes were eventually linked up to provide a through trolleybus service
** Joint through motor-bus service with Walsall Corporation from 4/2/29; converted to trolleybus 16/11/31
\# Motor-bus service subsequently converted to trolleybus
\#\# Linked-up motor-bus service; later separate trolleybus routes
\+ Motor-bus service (to Merry Hill 17/6/29-25/7/29); trolleybus from 27/10/30

Above: No 58, a Guy BTX, stands under the trees at Upper Green, Tettenhall, waiting to return to town, in the early 1930s. The road is the main A41 north to Whitchurch and Chester. *John Hughes collection*

2. Expansion in the 1930s

The 1930 Road Traffic Act heralded the introduction of Road Service Licences, Wolverhampton Corporation applying for and being granted 36. These were issued on 23 April 1931, when the application was considered at the first licensing session in Wolverhampton's Town Hall, 14 licences being allocated to trolleybus routes. Briefly, Wolverhampton now had the largest system in the world, having, at the end of 1930, 70 trolleybuses in operation over 10 routes, their apple-green and primrose livery being a familiar sight to visiting transport operators keen to view a successful system. The ensuing years were to see continuing expansion of the trolleybus system over and above the motor-bus network, with costs playing a dominant factor in decision policy. The General Manager's report of November 1930 stated that operating costs for trolleybuses were 13.85d per mile as against 15.74d per mile for motor buses. With the average income showing at 16d per mile the advantage was clearly with the trolleybus. In consequence the council placed a further order for 10 more trolleybuses to enable conversion of existing routes.

From 3 February 1930 Walsall Corporation suspended its tram service to Willenhall, a through motor-bus service to Wolverhampton starting the following day using single-deckers. This was done to allow the road under the railway bridge at Lower Horseley Fields, which carried the LMS main line to London Euston, to be lowered, the work being completed on 18 September 1930. Following this the canal bridge was realigned (on 7 November 1931), the trolleybus service to Willenhall being again suspended, from 27 April to 13 November, and seven motor buses hired from Guy and Sunbeam to cover the workings.

Traffic receipts having reached the levels required by the December 1927 agreement with Walsall Corporation, a through service of double-deck trolleybuses commenced on 16 November 1931, Walsall providing two of its trolleybuses for the joint route, having opened its first trolleybus route as far as Willenhall some months earlier. At the Walsall end of the route trolleybuses turned back using a traffic island at the top of Park Street in front of Her Majesty's Theatre, adjacent to Green Lane and Stafford Street. An unusual feature of this operation that continued to the very end was that each undertaking kept its trolleys grouped in line. However, trolleys on route 5 to Willenhall were intermingled with Walsall-bound vehicles, irrespective of ownership.

Roads underneath the many railway bridges around the town were successively lowered to allow the full operation of double-deck vehicles. Cannock Road had been dealt with by 16 August 1930, while the roadway beneath the bridge at Dunstall Park station reopened in lowered form on 9 May 1937. Also lowered at the same time was the road under the Victoria Basin Bridge; a little further into town, this had been a major cause of traffic congestion and was rebuilt with straight girder-work.

The year 1931 was to see the first Sunbeam trolleybus supplied from that firm's Moorfield works. An MS2 model with Weymann bodywork, it started as a demonstrator with the Corporation on 8 July and was taken into stock in June 1932, being allocated fleet number 95. All subsequent trolleybuses would be of Guy or Sunbeam manufacture.

At the 1931 Commercial Motor Show at Olympia the Gilford Motor Co (first registered on 6 November 1926 at premises in High Wycombe) provided an unusual exhibit that was to touch on Wolverhampton's trolleybus operation. A new design of double-deck bus, it was of chassisless construction, with a low floor (just 14in ground clearance) and independent suspension, power being provided by a licence-built six-cylinder Junkers engine driving the front wheels; fitted with a 50-seat metal-frame body by the Wickham Motor Body Co and featuring wraparound windows, the vehicle was built to a low overall height of 12ft 11in. Buyers were cautious, no orders being received, and, fitted with a 70hp ECC motor, it was converted as a trolleybus, still to no avail. Registered JW 2347 and painted in Wolverhampton livery, it finally entered service with the Corporation, running on loan as a demonstrator from 17 November to 31 December 1932, although it was never taken into stock. The demonstration period failed to attract any orders, and the Gilford Motor Co ceased trading on 31 November 1935, when a receiver was appointed. With liabilities of £21,802 and assets of just £5,720, the company was sold to the firm of HSG, which specialised in producer-gas vehicles.

On 30 November 1931 the motor-bus route to Bushbury Hill was converted to double-deck trolleybus operation as route 9A, the cross-town link with motor-bus route 13 to Merry Hill being severed as a result, the trolleybuses for Bushbury Hill starting from the town centre. Motor buses continued to operate from town to Merry Hill, running from Victoria Square, via Queen Street and Princes Square. The Merry Hill service had been introduced on 1 January 1925 to serve to new housing within the Borough boundary, being extended across town on 5 December 1927 to serve the Twelfth Avenue area, running from the George Hotel in Stafford Street via Park Lane, the extension to Bushbury Hill being added on 16 July 1928.

During 1932 the dedicated trolleybus journeys for Courtaulds' factory employees were revised as follows:

24 February	Five additional trips to town
	One additional trip to Merry Hill
	Two additional trips to 16th Avenue, Low Hill
30 May	One trip to 16th Avenue cancelled, the other extended to Showell Circus
10 October	One trip to town cancelled

Two further motor-bus routes were converted to trolleybus, on the northeast side of town. They were the 9 to Amos Lane and the 9B to Low Hill (Pear Tree), on 21 March 1932. The outer terminus for the Amos Lane route was alongside the Red Lion public house, where trolleybuses stopped on the far side of Prestwood Road crossroads before reversing to the right into Amos Lane and then turning left, back into Prestwood Road to return to town. The service was linked across town with route 12 to Bradmore and worked out via Great Brickkiln Street and Jeffcock Road to a reverser at Bradmore crossroads, giving the rare situation of a service with a reversing triangle at each end.

The Amos Lane route had its origins in a motor-bus service that started on 7 September 1911, running to the top of Victoria Road in Fallings Park at its junction with Bushbury Road, with later extensions to Prestwood Road and, by 16 July 1928, Amos Lane. It is possible that a reverser was used at Victoria Road when trolleybus services started, but by 18 October 1934 all trolleys were working through to Amos Lane, the wiring curve eventually being tied off to traction poles, though kept electrically live. A turning-circle was probably also used for a short period, at Prestwood Road Post Office. At Low Hill terminus a widened section of road at the County Borough boundary allowed a turning-circle to be constructed outside the Pear Tree public house adjacent to Pear Tree Lane, a short distance beyond the motor-bus terminus at Primrose Lane.

The service to Penn, operated by single-deck motor buses to the Rose & Crown since 20 May 1914, commenced operation on 10 October 1932 with double-deck trolleybuses. Wiring was extended from Penn Fields terminus along Stubbs Road (this having been devoid of a service since tram route 4 had been converted), then down Penn Road some way beyond the Rose & Crown to a new turning-circle at the town boundary. A short working, terminating in a turning-circle at the junction of Penn Road and Mount Road, adjacent to the Mount public house, was given route number 11, the service to/from the outer terminus being numbered 11A. The more direct route to Penn along the main road from its junction with Lea Road was also wired up but was initially held back for emergency workings only and consequently saw few vehicle movements.

The service was to be re-routed along the Penn Road direct wiring from 8 April 1935, following the Oxbarn Avenue 32 service as far as the junction with Coalway Road. Powers were also obtained to erect wires in Woodfield Avenue, though they were never used; Woodfield Avenue diverges from the Penn Road just beyond the Mount Road turn, and the tree-lined road with solid villa-style housing curves gently round to join up with Coalway Road, and a fairly lengthy turn-back would have been created as a result. At this time route 4 to Penn Fields was reintroduced, terminating as before at the Lea Road terminus. Stubbs Road was then used only on Sunday-morning services until 13 October 1936, from which date all Penn workings travelled via the direct route, the section in Stubbs Road falling out of use again, though retained *in situ*.

Additional cross-town workings were created on 10 April 1933, when further Bradmore services were converted to trolleybus. Services 12A and 13 left town by way of Chapel Ash and Merridale Road, joining service 12 at the junction of Jeffcock Road for the last mile to Bradmore. At the crossroads service 13 continued through Bradmore and down Trysull Road to its junction with Coalway Road, about ³/₄ mile further on.

Service 12A, nominally an extension of service 12, turned right at Bradmore. It ran along Broad Lane, traversing the western boundary of Bantock Park, and ended outside the New Inn public house, where another reversing triangle was used, trolleys turning left into Coppice Road and then reversing at an acute angle across the main Castlecroft Road to regain the near-side kerb, alongside the white-painted

walls of the pub; there was little room for error, and such a manœuvre would not be allowed today. In the opposite direction services 12A and 13 worked through to Low Hill via the 9B route. The conversions had been made possible as a result of existing powers plus new ones obtained in 1932. The Finchfield route had its origins in an early motor-bus service to Bradmore, introduced on 16 October 1919, and running from Skinner Street via Great Brickkiln Street, Rayleigh Road and Jeffcock Road; this was extended on 25 July 1928 to the New Inn in Finchfield, and on 10 January 1930 the town terminus moved to Queen Street.

On 11 June 1933 a through service was introduced from Wednesfield to Bushbury and Fordhouses via Wolverhampton town centre, linking services 6 and 6A with 3 and 3A. It proved to be short-lived, being withdrawn on 9 May 1937, the Bushbury and Fordhouses services then being linked up with service 9A to Bushbury Hill; no additional wiring was required, existing sections of route being used throughout. By 23 December the diversion wiring in Lower Stafford Street was operational, being used to avoid football traffic in Waterloo Road and provide direct special services for race meetings at Dunstall Park, the trolleys using the Greenwood Road loop to return to town.

Over the years many visitors came from towns, both in the UK and worldwide, to inspect the (by now) well-known trolleybus system in Wolverhampton and talk to its equally famous and supportive General Manager, Charles Owen Silvers. Most came with a view to assessing the mode of transport for use in their own towns, and

among these, late in 1933, was a substantial group of officers and councillors from Bournemouth, who, suitably impressed, decided to replace their tram system with trolleybuses.

On 10 February 1934 service 6A was extended to Wednesfield town centre, wires having been erected over the canal bridge and along High Street to a traffic island at the junction with Lichfield Road, by the Cross Guns public house. The destination blind for this route now read 'Wood End'. Two days later the last trolleybus service to be introduced in Wolverhampton commenced running. Allocated route number 32, it ran to Oxbarn Avenue via Coalway Road. Again, it replaced a motor-bus service, in this case introduced on 10 April 1932, from Market Street. From the beginning it used the direct line of wiring along Penn Road rather than follow the Penn 11A trolleys down Lea Road, through Penn Fields. After diverging at the Lea Road turn, it made a steady climb to a summit by the Royal Orphanage, following this with a brisk run downhill to the junction with Stubbs Road, where the Penn service rejoined Penn Road. Located on the downhill stretch was one of the red-painted compulsory stops, placed there to ensure that the temptation to speed was damped. At Coalway Road, a short way beyond Stubbs Road, the 32 service turned right through spring-loaded overhead pointwork, preset to Coalway Road, it being easier for the conductor of a trolleybus bound for Penn to operate the pull-cord for the points and jump back onto the rear platform of his trolley as it moved slowly over the crossroads. Leaving Penn Road behind, the

Above: Sunbeam MS2 trolleys 92-95, all with Weymann bodywork, pose for an official photograph outside Cleveland Road depot after delivery in 1932. *John Hughes collection*

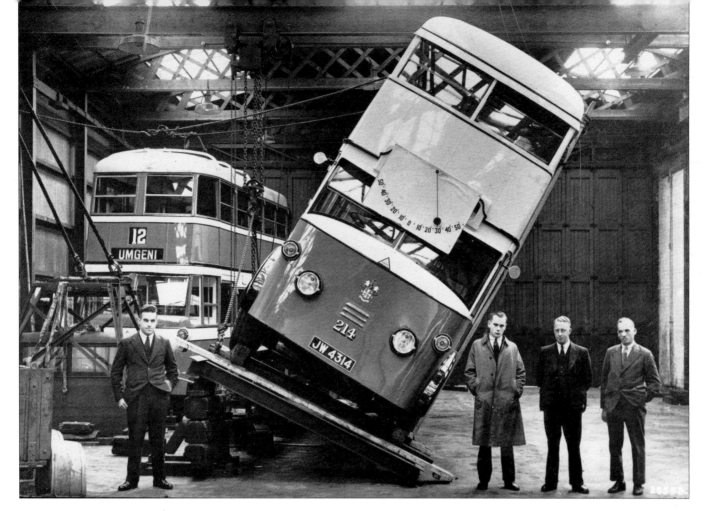

Above: The Sunbeam works at Moorfield Road in Wolverhampton, with Beadle-bodied Sunbeam MS3 214 undergoing a standard tilt test to gauge its stability. The trolley behind is part of an export order destined for Durban, South Africa. *John Hughes collection*

route ran gently downhill for some distance through an area of 1920s semi-detached private housing to terminate at the crossroads with Oxbarn Avenue and Warstones Road, where the wiring formed a loop around an elongated traffic island, almost within sight of the Merryhill terminus, half a mile away. Some consideration was given to extending the route just over $^1/_2$ mile down Coalway Road to link up with the terminus of route 13 at the Merry Hill traffic island, but the idea was not pursued. A similar suggestion was raised for linking up route 4 to services on the Jeffcock Road wires, though this too was not followed up. Had these suggestions been acted upon they would have strengthened the system considerably and improved the overall service provided to the public. A proposal in the 1936 Parliamentary Bill for powers to extend route 32 down Warstones Road to Springhill also failed.

The year 1934 saw the entry of another player in trolleybus manufacture in the form of the Rootes Group, which purchased Karrier Motors of Huddersfield and transferred production to Sunbeam, its Wolverhampton-based trolleybus-manufacturing subsidiary. In 1931 Sunbeam had branched out from car production in an attempt to diversify and avoid bankruptcy, only to be acquired by Rootes in 1934 after encountering severe financial problems and calling in the receivers. Sunbeam's

standard six-wheel trolleybus was the MS2. Wolverhampton was to take only 10 in total (including the prototype, in 1931), although nine of the low-framed MS3 models would be delivered before production was curtailed by the receivers.

Policy had been to place small orders for buses and trolleybuses (each being numbered in a separate series) as each conversion became due. Now, as vehicles came in for a repaint, at a rate of one per week, motor buses were renumbered by having 100 added to the existing fleet number, the trolleybus sequence moving to 200 after delivery of No 99.

August 1934 saw the arrival of a further Sunbeam MS2, latterly Birmingham Corporation No 67. A former demonstrator, with Metro-Cammell bodywork seating 59, it had run only 2,990 miles but was non-standard in the Birmingham fleet, hence the decision to sell it. Wolverhampton Corporation was quick to spot a bargain, and it was purchased for £1,850, being re-upholstered (for a further £65) before entering service. Numbered 222 in Wolverhampton's fleet, it was to give sterling service on the Tettenhall route for many years.

Victoria Square now acted as a main town terminus for several services, with

trolleys on routes 4 (Penn Fields), 11 (Mount Road), 11A (Penn) and 32 (Oxbarn Avenue) loading on the central reservation in the middle of the square; although dangerous-sounding, this tended to keep both trolleys and passengers clear of the traffic flow around the perimeter.

As already mentioned, a small change was effected on 8 October, when the Fighting Cocks terminus for trolleybuses from Wolverhampton was moved a few hundred yards south to Dudding Road, where provision for two bays was made in the overhead wiring; this allowed inbound workings from Dudley to by-pass those trolleys terminating at Dudding Road. Trolleys on route 25 from Willenhall continued to turn at the Fighting Cocks junction, a new traffic island being constructed here to facilitate this. On 12 December 1934 the Greenwood Road loop was lifted, the short-working terminus of the Fordhouses route being moved a short distance further north along Stafford Road to a new turning-circle at Church Road, Oxley.

In 1936 there arrived a further batch of three Sunbeam MF1 single-deck trolleys, the first of which, No 231, had been exhibited at the 1935 Commercial Motor Show at Earl's Court. On the debit side 31

Above: Victoria Square in August 1937. No 222, a Sunbeam MS2 demonstrator with a Metro-Cammell body, arrives from Tettenhall. This trolleybus was purchased in September 1934 from Birmingham Corporation, being non-standard to that fleet. It is followed here by 226, another Sunbeam MS2, purchased new in 1935. *Author's collection*

October saw the withdrawal from service of Guy BTX No 33. This was then re-purchased by Guy Motors, which intended to preserve it, but unfortunately it had to be scrapped due to financial difficulties encountered during World War 2.

Increased usage by Courtaulds employees saw a further addition to the dedicated trolleybus services, an extra working to Showell Circus being instigated with effect from Tuesday 12 January 1936. This was followed on 6 September by a relocation of the route 25 Fighting Cocks terminus to Dudding Road, where it re-joined route 8, plus 8A and 8B in the purpose-built layover bays.

At the beginning of 1937 six TIM machines from the Ticket Issuing Machine Co Ltd were successfully trialled, and in due course orders were placed for 130 machines, these replacing some of the equipment then on hire from the Bell Punch Co.

Following the completion on 10 May 1937 of road-lowering at the Stafford Road railway bridge, routes 3 and 3A to Fordhouses were linked up with route 9A (as described previously) to form a new cross-town service to Bushbury Hill. Through-running from Fordhouses to Wednesfield was discontinued, and services 6 and 6A from Wednesfield now turned in the town centre using newly erected wiring in Thornley Street and Westbury Street, leaving the Wednesfield route to its own devices.

Wrottesley Park, on the main road to Shifnal and Albrighton, was the venue chosen for the 1937 Royal Agricultural Show, held from 6 to 10 July, and a regular, direct motor-bus service, numbered 1A, was laid on from the railway station in Wolverhampton. Connecting with the Tettenhall trolleybus terminus and serving an expanding area further along the Wergs Road, it was well placed to assist with the additional traffic generated by the show, and a considerably increased frequency of existing motor buses helped to handle the burgeoning crowds arriving by trolleybus at Tettenhall terminus, a mile or so short of the park.

Further alterations took place in the Bradmore area on 8 November 1937, when wires in the lower half of Jeffcock Road, connecting it with Merridale Road, were taken out of use. They remained *in situ* for many years, being used by driver-training vehicles until disconnected at the Merridale Road end *c*1944 and removed altogether when new 2ft line-hangers were installed on routes 9 and 12. From 8 November the realigned routes were operated as shown below.

The Finchfield service, running via Merridale Road, combined with route 13 to give a frequency in of 10 trolleys per hour instead of the previous six, this being necessary to handle the extra capacity created by new housing development in the Finchfield and Merry Hill areas. Service 12 from Amos Lane to Bradmore was cut back at both ends to run from town (Railway Street) via Great Brickkiln Street to the junction of Jeffcock Road and Downham Place, terminating at a newly installed reverser, the Pear Tree–Finchfield through service being effectively discontinued.

During 1937/8 a new depot and offices were erected in Park Lane, opposite the Guy Motors works on the northeast side of Wolverhampton, on route 9A to Bushbury. Totalling 15 1/2 acres, the land, in various lots, was purchased in 1936 for £3,100. Design work was dealt with during that year, and a contract for construction awarded to H. J. Amies & Son Ltd of Wolverhampton in March 1937, for the sum of £31,090. Tarmac roadways and extensive external perimeter trolley wiring, at an additional cost of £2,900, allowed vehicle testing within the

9B Low Hill — cross-town — 13 Merry Hill, running every 10 minutes

9 Amos Lane — cross-town — 12A Finchfield, running every 15 minutes

12 Bradmore — Jeffcock Road — Wolverhampton, running every 15 minutes

depot site, on what was effectively a mini trolleybus system. Unusually the overhead layout took trolleybuses on an anti-clock-wise circuit around the depot, the wiring at the entrance/exit being erected so as to place trolleys firmly on the right-hand side of the road. As soon as the depot was completed on 25 July 1938, trolleys covering the Bushbury Hill–Fordhouses route were moved down from Cleveland Road depot, as were those on services 9, 9B, 12, 12A and 13, the 6 and 6A following on 31 October. Motor-bus services would be transferred on 1 May 1939, the official handover ceremony not being held until 6 October.

On 12 September 1938 double-deck trolleys replaced the single-deckers on the Fordhouses–Bushbury service, as a conse-quence of the lowering of the carriageway (completed 9 May 1937) underneath the railway bridges adjacent to the Stafford Road Works and Dunstall Park station, on the Fordhouses section of the route. This left the Wednesfield route as the system's sole remaining single-deck trolleybus serv-ice. The move from Cleveland Road freed up sufficient space to allow the transfer from Sedgley depot of all trolleys servicing the Dudley route, which in turn permitted the final closure of Sedgley depot, on 31 October.

In January 1939 another report was issued by the General Manager on the run-ning costs of vehicles in his care. On this occasion it was stated that manufacturers' continuing development of the oil (diesel) engine had resulted in motor buses' show-ing a slightly lower overall operating cost

Above: **Official photograph of Park Royal-bodied 245, a Sunbeam MS2 delivered in 1936.** *Author's collection*

than that of trolleybuses. Notwithstanding this, it was agreed that the status quo would remain, with continued faith in the trolleybus fleet, the Transport Committee keeping the report for future reference.

By March agreement had been reached with the management of the Courtaulds factory that the ongoing payment of £2 per week per vehicle towards the provision of workers' trolleybus services into its premis-es would cease with effect from 1 April 1940, Courtaulds having felt for some time that, with the overall increase in such traffic around the town already being pro-

vided at the Transport Department's expense, it was, due to an historical prece-dent, being unfairly singled out.

In April a request by the Urban District Council in Wednesfield for an extension of the Amos Lane route beyond the reverser and along Lower Prestwood Road to the Pheasant Inn was approved in principle. However, due to various unrelated issues (including a road-widening scheme) early action was not possible, and the extension — the last to be made to Wolverhampton's system — would not become fully opera-tional until 25 June 1956.

Roe-bodied Guy BT 259, delivered in 1938, seen in a mainly green livery at Penn terminus. Note the old-style telephone box on the corner. *John Hughes collection*

3. The War Years

From the mid-1930s the unstable political situation in Europe had begun to deteriorate as Germany, under the yoke of the Nazi party and its leader, Adolf Hitler, rose to power and began making intimidating threats towards its European neighbours. Following the annexation of Czechoslovakia by Germany in 1938 Hitler began, in March 1939, to press Poland into permitting the construction of new road and rail links across its territories to improve communications between East Prussia and Germany. The annexation had breached a written assurance by Hitler that had been handed to British Prime Minister Neville Chamberlain in Munich in 1938, at which meeting both Britain and France had reluctantly endorsed the forced transfer of the ethnically German Sudetenland from Czechoslovakia to Germany. The British Government, increasingly concerned by events unfolding, then issued a formal guarantee of Poland's borders on 31 March 1939, with a rider that they expected Hitler to moderate his demands.

With the possibility of Britain being drawn into a conflict, instructions were initiated by the Government to industry and commerce, and various preparatory steps were taken. Air Raid Precaution (ARP) instructions had already been issued in October 1938, and in Wolverhampton two Transport Department Traffic Inspectors were detailed for training as ARP Instructors, together with 12 staff to be trained in decontamination work. After Sedgley depot closed, the Urban District Council requested its use for Civil Defence and first-aid use, the building being leased to it for this purpose. To protect depot staff in the event of an air raid part of the basement at Cleveland Road depot was turned into a shelter. A pit was similarly converted at Bilston, while at Park Lane new underground shelters were constructed.

Transport staff were encouraged to join the Territorial Army, and many enlisted. By September 1939 some 85 staff across all grades, including 31 drivers and 44 conductors, had been 'called to the colours', these representing nearly 11% of the total staff. It was an admirable gesture on the part of those who went to serve, and the Transport Department struggled to maintain services as the rate of call-up adversely affected the supply of conductors available for driver training. As had been the case in World War 1, many women came forward in response to requests to work as both conductors and drivers. First Aid classes were arranged for staff in July, while black-out trials on buildings took place in August, and shaded bulbs, giving only a weak light, were fitted inside all buses and trolleybuses.

The fear of war finally became a reality at 6am on 1 September 1939, when the Polish capital Warsaw was struck by the first of a succession of bombing raids (the Blitzkrieg) while two major German army groups invaded Poland from Prussia in the north and Slovakia in the South. At 8am Poland requested military assistance from Britain and France, but it was not until noon on 3 September that Britain declared war on Germany (to be followed at 5pm by France), the delay reflecting the somewhat naïve hope that Hitler would respond to demands and end the invasion. The decision to go to war having been made, Chamberlain broadcast the following statement by radio to the British nation:

"This morning the British Ambassador in Berlin handed the German Government a final note, stating that, unless we heard from them by eleven o'clock that they were prepared at once to withdraw their troops from Poland, a state of war would exist between us. I have to tell you now that no such undertaking has been received, and that consequently this country is at war with Germany."

One immediate consequence of the declaration was the termination of all services after the 10pm departure each evening, rather than the usual 11pm. This came into operation from 6 September in an early move to introduce economies, whereby a number of less essential motor-bus services were withdrawn completely. All services were reduced in frequency, any motor-bus services that duplicated trolley-bus workings being withdrawn. With the uncertainty of future availability in mind, the Transport Committee authorised the bulk purchase of a number of stores/maintenance items, including several months' stock of brake liners, suspension springs and lubricating oil. Also purchased were a year's supply of overhead fittings, together with 10 miles of trolleybus wire and 24 gross of trolley wheels (up to 60 per week could be used). By November it had been agreed to relax the timing of the last departure slightly, one extra journey running on most routes between 10.15 and 10.20pm.

Christmas 1939 passed uneventfully, but at the end of January 1940 the town was gripped by a severe snowstorm, followed by alternate thaw and frost, which compounded the misery as people struggled to go about their daily business. Roads became treacherous and unusable, the salt put down having little effect, and the resultant icy potholes causing many broken bus springs. With conditions worsening, the Transport Department reluctantly took the unpalatable but sensible decision to cease operating, and on 5 February all trolleybuses and motor buses returned to their depots, where they were to remain until 8 February, by which time it was possible to restore a full service.

The opportunity had been taken during December and January to erect a section of single wiring along Waterloo Road between Molineux Street and the junction with Newhampton Road, a feeder point being installed at the Molineux Street junction from the Bushbury-route supply. This is presumed to have been a safety measure, so that, in the event of air-raid damage, an alternative route out of town for northbound trolleys serving factories essential for the war effort could be quickly put into operation. Once erected it remained tied off at each end to traction poles and disconnected from the electricity supply.

The summer of 1940 was to see the German Luftwaffe attempt to win air superiority over southern Britain and the English Channel by destroying the Royal Air Force and the British aircraft industry. The Battle of Britain, as it became known, was fought in the skies over England between 10 July and 31 October, and in those 114 dark days 544 brave young airmen, including volunteers from the Commonwealth and the USA, lost their lives in the attempt to keep the skies of Britain free. As Winston Churchill was to say in Parliament during his famous speech on 20 August, right in the middle of concerted German air attacks on southern Britain, "Never in the field of human conflict has so much been owed by so many to so few". Following Fighter Command's success in defeating the German attempt the Luftwaffe changed tactics in the autumn and began saturation night bombing of London, over 76 consecutive nights, together with major ports and industrial centres across Britain in an unsuccessful attempt to bring the country to its knees.

Havoc was wrought on trolleybus services in London's East End and at the ports of Cardiff, Kingston-upon-Hull and Portsmouth, areas of the country all vital to the war effort, where overhead-repair gangs often worked around the clock to restore damaged stretches of wiring. Trolleys were frequently stranded for days at a time on sections of otherwise good overhead, due to a combination of bomb

craters, unexploded bombs and fire-damaged buildings collapsing onto the roadway. By contrast Wolverhampton, despite being located on the edge of the industrial 'Black Country', suffered less disruption to its services and escaped much of the devastation that was suffered elsewhere.

In the event of an air-raid warning sounding, crews, in liaison with the Police, were given discretion to keep services running for as long as was practicable. Notices were issued advising on such things as the carrying of gas masks on duty and the need for conductors to take under their care children travelling unattended on a bus or trolleybus during an air raid. The need was emphasised to pass under insulators and frogs with the power pedal off, to avoid flashes, as was the requirement — where possible — to park up trolleys at least 20 yards apart during air raids. The shortage of staff available to man vehicles was eased slightly when the Ministry of Labour agreed to make public transport a reserved occupation, thus ensuring that employees could not resign or move to other work unless first cleared to do so by the Ministry. Further easing of crew shortages was achieved by allowing drivers to remain in employment with the Transport Department beyond the normal retirement age of 65.

The war was to affect every aspect of British life, operation of the trolleybus system being no exception. As holiday traffic around the country diminished many South Coast seaside towns were able to operate with smaller fleets, and for the duration, with Government approval, a number of trolleybuses were sent north from Bournemouth, Brighton, Hastings and Portsmouth to assist with the additional needs of industrial towns and cover the shortfall where manufacturers were unable to meet deliveries on existing orders. Indirectly this also served a further purpose, as that part of Southern England had been designated a prohibited area due to its proximity to France and the very real possibility of Hitler's 'Operation Sea Lion' invasion taking place.

In 1939 Wolverhampton had placed orders for 10 new trolleybuses and six new motor buses, the Regional Traffic Commissioner initially granting approval for the manufacturers to obtain the licences for construction from the Ministry of Transport. Subsequent withdrawal of approval for the motor buses, coupled with general delays, meant that the obsolete trolleybuses intended for withdrawal would probably not last the course until the arrival of new vehicles. The General Manager then made urgent enquiries with other undertakings and was able to report back to the September 1940 Committee meeting that he had been successful in locating a suitable supply of trolleybuses that could be loaned. After further consultation with the Mayor and the Chairman of the Transport Committee, approval to proceed was quickly given.

Agreement had been reached between the Corporation and that of Bournemouth to hire 12 trolleybuses at an annual rate of £240 each. Arrangements were made with the Sunbeam company to tow the trolleys at a cost of £21 each, and between 4 September and 10 December 1940 12 of Bournemouth's Sunbeam MS2 trolleys went 'home' to Wolverhampton, a further two vehicles (Nos 78 and 79) going to nearby Walsall; other Bournemouth trolleys were despatched to Newcastle, South Shields, Llanelly and London. These trolleybuses were fitted with Park Royal dual-entrance/exit bodywork with front and rear staircases. This was not a problem in Newcastle, where the standard internal layout was similar to that of the nine vehicles hired in, but elsewhere, including Wolverhampton, the front entrance doors officially remained closed during their stay, only the conventional rear open platform being used: in practice, a blind eye was often turned to this instruction, drivers making full use of the new facility. The hired trolleys, all with BTH traction equipment, went straight into service on routes 9B and 13 and were to remain in Wolverhampton until the end of World War 2. Two of the Bournemouth trolleys, Nos 76 and 84, were renumbered (as 176 and 184) during the hire period, but the remainder retained their Bournemouth fleet numbers throughout their stay in Wolverhampton.

Further negotiations with Bournemouth Corporation resulted in the hiring of 20 drivers and conductors to crew the vehicles, the men receiving their standard wages plus an additional allowance of 3s 6d per night to cover lodging expenses, although a lack of suitable accommodation, coupled with reluctance on the part of the Ministry of Labour to cover the lodging allowance, saw a number of crews subsequently return to Bournemouth.

Whereas Bournemouth's trolleybuses retained their colourful primrose and maroon livery, most of the vehicles supplied to Wolverhampton between 1939 and 1945 were, in common with those of other operators, painted in wartime grey, those new in 1944 (Nos 402-7) also being fitted with wooden slatted seats. Headlights were fitted with hoods, reducing the amount of light being emitted to minimise the chance of being picked up by enemy aircraft.

The outbreak of World War 2 had caused problems to pile up rapidly for passenger-transport operators, labour and materials being in increasingly short supply. Standards of maintenance began to fall due to the excessively high mileages being worked, although this was reduced by a lack of crews and vehicles. With passenger numbers and revenue increasing an order was placed in May 1940 for 10 new trolleybuses, this being followed in 1941 by an order for 20 new motor buses. The trolleybuses were to be Sunbeam MF2 models, fitted with Park Royal bodywork. Also ordered in 1941 was a new Guy Vixen tower wagon, to supplement the three Tilling-Stevens vehicles, which had been converted from buses some years back and were proving increasingly unreliable, but intervention by the MoWT resulted in a Fordson vehicle being approved instead.

The first months of the new year saw similar wintry conditions to those experienced one year earlier, in January 1940, with blizzard conditions disrupting all traffic. Lessons learned from the previous year saw emergency arrangements activated, with services maintained on all town workings. Some country bus routes were out of action for several days, however, with snowdrifts several feet deep cutting off a number of villages, but by 1 February all services were back to normal.

The strain imposed on the transport network by wartime conditions meant that the system was now being worked to the limit and operating at the very edge of its capability. At the March meeting of the Transport Committee the General Manager graphically illustrated this by pointing out that 24 vehicles were now running in service with unacceptable body damage — a situation that, for safety reasons, at the very least, would not be tolerated in peacetime — and that this, coupled with a backlog of overdue maintenance on chassis and motors, meant that the spectre of multiple vehicle failure was never far away. The Committee deferred a decision on fare increases until October, in the event deciding not to sanction this.

With effect from Monday 7 July 1941 two evening trips from the Courtaulds factory, one each to Merry Hill and Showell Circus, had been withdrawn, it being felt that the existing timetable could handle the volume of traffic without undue strain being placed on the system.

During the summer months late-night workings on all trolleybus routes were extended to 11pm, in an effort to alleviate conditions for the travelling public and to assist local business. In October the Transport Committee resolved to cut back the last workings to 9.30pm. The local cinemas were at that stage closing at 10pm as agreed between the Ministry of Home Security and the Chief Constable for the area. Further discussions were entered into with the Regional Transport Commissioner, and agreement was given for trolleybuses to operate until 10.30pm, but motor-bus routes still had to finish at 9.30pm.

The 10 Sunbeam/Park Royal trolleybuses ordered in 1940 arrived during 1942 and were put straight into service as Nos 286-95. The Transport Department then requested a further 12 trolleybuses as being necessary to maintain services, but the MoWT allocated only a further six, contracts being placed with Sunbeam. Numbered 296-9 and 400/1, they were the first of the wartime utility type with Weymann MoWT-style bodies and were delivered, in grey livery, during July and August 1943.

By 1942 only one manufacturer of trolleybus chassis was approved by the Ministry of Supply and the Ministry of War Transport, the Sunbeam works at Wolverhampton being authorised to produce a 'standardised' design that would be suitable for all users. This was the Sunbeam / Karrier W4. Of two-axle design, it had traction motors positioned so as to permit the use of lowbridge bodies. Utility-style bodies would come from Weymann, Park Royal and Brush, motors of 80-85hp, being supplied by BTH, English Electric, Metropolitan Vickers and General Electric. After Daimler's Radford works were destroyed in the German air-raid blitz of Coventry the Government moved quickly to ensure that production of bus chassis could be resumed, and in December 1942 Daimler was allowed to use space in the Courtaulds complex; this meant that virtually all wartime output of bus and trolleybus chassis from Daimler, Guy and Sunbeam/Karrier was produced in Wolverhampton.

Alterations to town termini on 23 February included moving the Tettenhall loading bay in Victoria Square to a loop installed outside the GPO in Lichfield Street. Service 11A to Penn was also moved from Victoria Square and now loaded in Railway Street, this being made practical by running anti-clockwise via Broad Street and Princess Square, thus regaining Lichfield Street on the outward-bound journey.

At the time of its loan of 12 trolleybuses Bournemouth Corporation had also agreed to sell a quantity of unused traction poles to Wolverhampton, on the understanding that, should they ever be needed in Bournemouth, an equivalent number would be provided in return. These were intended for use on the proposed extension of the Fordhouses route to the Boulton Paul aircraft factory at Pendeford, but concerns from the company and Air Ministry that flashes at night from the wiring could guide German bombers meant that this was never erected, and 65 poles were returned to Bournemouth during 1942.

On 31 July 1942 the Walsall service was disrupted near Coventry Street as a result of 'enemy action' whereby high explosive bombs fell in Willenhall Road, bringing down the trolley wires. Considerable rewiring and erection of traction poles was needed after removal of all the building rubble, and a shuttle service operated on either side of the damage, a full service not being resumed until 21 August, as high-tension wires had also been brought down at Portobello, adding to the problem. To facilitate the operation, jump leads were fashioned using two lengths of suitable cable attached at each end to the hooks on spare retriever poles; with the trolley booms lowered and secured, one retriever was hooked to the end of a trolley boom, and at the other end of each cable the second retriever was looped onto the overhead wire, enabling the trolley to draw power and move some way off the alignment while making a three-point turn. While all this was taking place, an emergency through service was put into action and operated via Bilston, making good use of the existing wiring on routes 7 and 25.

On the same day in July incendiary bombs were dropped in the early hours around the depots in Cleveland Road and Park Lane; evidently German intelligence had good knowledge of both the content and importance of the depot buildings. Business premises across the way from Cleveland Road depot were totally destroyed, but little or no damage was sustained by either depot building or by overhead wiring in the immediate vicinity. Buses dispersed to neighbouring streets also escaped unscathed. Because of the damage Cleveland Road depot was closed for the morning to allow clearance work to take place, but this did not stop the early services from being operated in full.

With effect from November 1942 bus and trolleybus services were stopped at 9pm each night. A restricted service, for workers only, continued up to 10.15pm, and people wishing to use this service were granted special permits issued through their employer. Early 1943 saw an improvement provided by Dudley Council to the Dudley terminus, when an area of wasteland adjacent to the Saracen's Head public house was made available and a much larger turning-circle installed; the Council also provided new waiting shelters at the improved terminus. For three days from 9 June 1943 the service to Whitmore Reans faced some disruption, excavation work in Hunter Street resulting in all trolleys' being forced to use route 2A in order to maintain the service.

The last of the low bridges around town, at Broad Street, was now dealt with, funding of £6,000 having been sought late in 1942 from the Ministry of Supply and the Ministry of War Transport. A grant was eventually agreed, and work commenced in September 1943. The road underneath was lowered for half its width and partially reopened on 29 November. Although double-deck vehicles were used on route 6A from this date, the road lowering was not completed until 17 February 1944, the opportunity being taken to replace the ancient trolley wiring to allow the use of skate collectors, fitted in March 1945.

By 1943 it was evident that the war was at last turning in favour of the Allies, and the Council began to consider just what would be needed to put the transport system back on its feet once the war had ended. The Transport Committee again considered the 1939 report on replacing trolleybuses with motor buses but, bearing in mind the probable oil supply problems that would be encountered for several years after the end of hostilities, together with the attendant costs, wisely decided to retain their faith in the trolleybus system. As a consequence an order was placed for 69 new trolleybuses and just 28 new motor buses.

The beginning of 1945 saw yet another bout of bad weather conditions, with severe frosts affecting the trolley wires and overhead equipment generally, but despite the snowfalls most roads were kept open, and services maintained. With the increasing likelihood of an end to the war in Europe Wolverhampton's Transport Committee again turned its attention to the future of its transport system, and the General Manager was asked to update his reports of January 1939 and March 1943. A new report was presented in March 1945 which drew attention to the fact that the overhead wiring was quite elderly in relation to the more modern trolleybuses using it, the design dating back to the mid-1920s. On the basis that the life of the existing system would be at least 10 years, approval was given to spend £20,000 on new wiring and brackets, together with feeder cables and electrically operated points. A programme to convert all trolley wheels to skate-type collectors was also agreed.

Following information and guidance received from the Ministry of Transport, authority was also given to place orders for 15 new trolleybuses and five new motor buses, to be allocated from the 1945/6 national programme, for delivery during 1946. July 1945 would see the expiry of powers from the 1932 and 1936 Acts to construct a number of trolleybus extensions, and a further extension of time was sought. The proposed extensions included Oxbarn Avenue, linking routes 32 and 13, Fryer Street, in the town centre, and an extension of the Finchfield route to Castlecroft.

Following the suicide of Adolf Hitler on 30 April hostilities came to an end on 5 May 1945. Hitler's successor, Admiral Karl Dönitz, sent General Alfred Jodl to offer an unconditional surrender to the Allied forces on 7 May in Rheims, France, German radio broadcasting that the general would sign the official surrender of Nazi Germany the following day. On hearing this Prime Minister Winston Churchill immediately announced that 8 May would be a national holiday, which would see the end of the war in Europe celebrated with street parties in towns and cities across the country.

The area around Buckingham Palace was a sea of people, all anxious to catch a glimpse of the King and Queen. At 3pm King George VI and Queen Elizabeth appeared on the balcony, to be joined by Mr Churchill, who delighted everyone present, waving to the crowds below and giving his by now famous 'V for Victory' sign. The date became known forever as VE (Victory in Europe) Day. Both 8 and 9 May were indeed celebrated as national holidays, and in Wolverhampton arrangements were made to operate bank-holiday-style services for both trolleybus and motor-bus routes on the days either side of this. A full service was operated on the first celebration day, but only until 5pm, as a gesture to allow staff to join in the festivities. All staff received full pay, additional monies being paid to those who had to work during the celebrations.

Above: Trolley 408, a Sunbeam F4, in Wulfruna Street on route 3A to Fordhouses. This was the only one of its batch (408-18) to be fitted with a Weymann body, the rest receiving Park Royal bodies. All would be rebodied by Park Royal in the 1950s. *John Hughes collection*

4. The Golden Years

With a gradual return to normality now possible, some tidying up of the assets was done, including the sale of the old tramway depot at Sedgley to the Urban District Council. The supply of trolleybuses was now improving, and authority was given to spend £30,000 on new vehicles to be placed in service as soon as conditions allowed.

In April 1946 the General Manager laid in front of the Transport Committee a report outlining plans for a major renewal of the fleet, for which the sum of £234,000 was approved. A number of services that had been withdrawn for the duration of hostilities were steadily reinstated, and the Corporation was ready to commence in earnest its programme of reinvestment, orders approved by the Transport Committee being placed for 46 new trolleybuses and 19 new motor buses, subsequently increased to 52 and 30 respectively. The plan was based around a final fleet figure of 157 trolleybuses and 95 motor buses, plus two tower wagons.

The General Manager's report had assumed that the Bournemouth trolleybuses would remain available for use in Wolverhampton for some time after the cessation of hostilities, but Bournemouth made an urgent request for their return, and by agreement five vehicles and their crews returned home in 1946, the balance following during the course of 1948, although No 129 appeared reluctant to go, not departing until December. Before leaving all were given a thorough overhaul and repainted, returning to Bournemouth in almost-new condition. Several of these trolleys went on to have extremely long lives by the sea, Nos 84, 105, 129, 131 and 168 still running as late as 1962.

Fleet number	Date hired out	Date returned
76	04/09/1940	26/10/1948
84	07/09/1940	03/06/1946
105	09/09/1940	17/07/1946
107	13/09/1940	28/06/1948
129	17/09/1940	07/12/1948
130	20/09/1940	19/07/1948
131	24/09/1940	28/05/1946
132	27/09/1940	02/07/1948
137	03/10/1940	01/11/1948
156	16/10/1940	22/07/1946
161	24/10/1940	20/05/1946
168	10/10/1940	27/07/1948

A request was also made in April to the Regional Transport Commissioner for approval to operate 8ft-wide vehicles on all motor-bus and trolleybus routes. The decision agreeing to this was reached in September, but permission was refused for the trolleybus routes to Dudley and Wednesfield and for the Fighting Cocks–Willenhall section. This made the application somewhat impractical, and as a result all vehicles delivered in 1947 were 7ft 6in wide.

The Bradmore group of trolleybus services appeared to be somewhat fated, as the cross-town operation was reorganised for the third time on 13 May 1946; service 12A to Finchfield was disconnected from its cross-town inter-working with service 9 to Amos Lane, service 12 to Jeffcock Road being linked up (again) with the existing service 9 as a cross-town working to Amos Lane. This resulted in a partial reversion to arrangements of 1932 and once more provided a cross-town service with a reverser at each end. Those journeys to Low Hill on service 9B that had, on returning, terminated in the town centre (instead of running through to Merry Hill on service 13) were now extended to form the new Finchfield service (12A). From the same date new wiring in Whitmore Street allowed westbound services arriving in town from Amos Lane to turn out of the busy Stafford Street to a quieter and less congested load-

Above: Sunbeam MF2 295 at Newbridge on 22 May 1946, having plunged down the embankment into a garden overlooking the GWR Wombourne branch. *Deryk Vernon collection*

ing point, Westbury Street and Broad Street being used to exit and regain Lichfield Street. The subject of extensions came up again when Tettenhall UDC requested that the Finchfield service be extended to Bhylls Lane, which road it was planning to widen to meet the needs of new housing. The request was approved, but the extension was not effected, a new motor-bus service beginning instead in 1949.

On 22 May 1946 disruption was caused in Newbridge, Tettenhall, when trolleybus 295 lost its footing and, leaving the road, plunged downhill through a fence, toppling into a garden at a lower level alongside the GWR railway line to Wombourne. The trolley came to rest pointing down at a steep angle with the rear wheels still on the pavement. Driver Hubbard escaped through the cab door and assisted Conductor Cahill in helping the 10 shaken passengers out of the trolley and back up the embankment. Two Burrell steam traction engines, *Mabon* and *Goliath*, were hired in from Pat Collins' travelling funfair, together with heavy lifting equipment, to secure recovery of the trolley in a remarkably unscathed condition, the damaged fencing being replaced afterwards. In a further incident, on 22 November, trolley 295 overturned yet again, this time at Bradmore. Fortunately no serious injuries resulted from either incident.

During 1946 the wiring in Stubbs Road received attention from the overhead linesmen, the pointwork at each end of the road, out of use since 13 October 1936, being removed. The wiring at Lea Road island was tied off to the traction poles in conventional fashion using insulators, but the Penn Road end was fixed in the form of a square crossing, terminating against the Penn Road wires (in which state it was to remain until shortly before the withdrawal of Penn Road trolleybuses, in 1963). Although physically isolated it could be quickly energised in the event of its being required, but some skill in driving was needed to counter the lack of gravity assistance when turning at the Penn Road end. At the same time short workings to Mount Road were reduced in frequency as the need to operate them decreased, such journeys ultimately ceasing altogether.

The first few weeks of 1947 saw atrocious weather conditions, including one of the worst snowfalls recorded in living memory, with drifts as deep as 20ft in some areas. The snowfall started on 24 January and continued intermittently until 4 March, by which time many villages were cut off, with more than 20 buses and snowploughs stranded, the conditions rendering any immediate rescue attempt impossible. For close on six weeks there had been freezing temperatures day and night, and fuel of any sort was virtually unobtainable. The Transport Department

services were overwhelmed, many routes being simply unable to operate. The trolleybuses, with their overhead equipment, were especially vulnerable and ceased running altogether in outlying areas.

The Transport and Highways departments made good use of the knowledge gained during World War 2 and more or less managed to keep the town routes open. A thick blanket of snow had built up against the depot doors, and German prisoners of war, still awaiting repatriation, were drafted in to assist in clearing the roads, huge walls of snow building up along the gutters as roads were progressively cleared. This in turn would reveal a perennial problem as temperatures rose, the slush and wet roads affecting the trolleys' insulation, resulting in passengers' getting mild electric shocks when holding on to the platform poles, the only remedy being to return the trolleybus to the depot until it had dried out.

As weather conditions slowly improved it emerged that 39 vehicles had sustained body damage, and overall mileage was down by 11%. With all services now functioning again special trolleybuses, fitted with ice-cutters, were kept running through the night to keep the wires from icing up in the sub-zero temperatures, and the use of ice-cutters subsequently became common practice on the first vehicles of the day when there had been icy conditions the previous night. As an example of the severity of that winter, the time allotted for vehicles travelling from Wolverhampton to Bilston was 60 minutes, as against the usual 13 minutes.

The first postwar trolleybuses to be delivered started arriving in April 1947. Ordered in September 1945, they were Sunbeam W chassis with Park Royal bodywork and were numbered 434-55. Guy Motors resumed production in 1946, supplying six Arab motor buses and a further 15 two-axle trolleybuses to Wolverhampton in 1947, plus 70 three-axle trolleybuses to Belfast.

On 12 September 1947 the decision was taken to relocate the remaining central loading bays in Victoria Square to the adjacent side streets. A move that was to affect all routes entering the town centre, it was implemented on 27 October. Construction of an additional wiring layout, originally authorised under the 1932 Act, allowed incoming services 4 and 32 to be worked via Fryer Street into Chubb Street alongside the Chubb Lock Works building, originally built for the Chubb brothers in 1889. The exit was via Railway Street and Victoria Square to regain Lichfield Street. The entry into Chubb Street and exit into Railway Street toward Victoria Square was a very tight one for trolleybuses, the overhead wiring having two equally tight parking-loops in Chubb Street itself. Applications continued to be

made periodically to the Ministry of Transport for time extensions to the powers granted to construct trolleybus routes until they were finally allowed to lapse on 11 July 1961.

Late in 1947 three EEC traction motors were purchased from Llanelly & District, but a proposal, made at this time, to obtain surplus trolleybuses was not followed up, these being considered unsuitable for use in Wolverhampton.

During the summer of 1948 the power station in Commercial Road received two new 750kV mercury arc rectifiers at a cost of £11,760, replacing the four rotary converter units, now over 30 years old, although one of the latter was retained for standby use. This was expected to reduce electricity consumption by up to 10% with improved efficiency.

A continuing postwar shortage of manpower and materials was still affecting production rates and the delivery of new vehicles originally promised for June, with every indication that those due towards the end of the year would be delayed by at least six to eight months. To maintain services and give the Transport Department any chance of increasing frequencies it became necessary to hire a number of coaches from local companies, including 14 vehicles supplied by local operator Don Everall. From 3 November 26 coaches began operating peak-time supplemental journeys across the system, the number of vehicles allocated to the trolleybus routes being as follows: 7 (2), 8B (5), 13 (4), 25 (2), 3A (4).

Additional capacity was provided on the cross-town service between Fordhouses and Bushbury Hill by using Worthington's 28- and 32-seat Bedford OWB vehicles. The number of coaches and suppliers was gradually reduced as conditions improved, but it would be July 1949 before the Transport Department had sufficient vehicle cover to be able to release all the remaining coaches back to their respective owners.

Notwithstanding the setback of 1946, the Transport Department had continued to push for complete acceptance of 8ft-wide trolleybuses, and on 3 September 1948 Wolverhampton's first such vehicles — part of a batch of 26 Sunbeam F4s — finally entered service. In November another, 479, enjoyed a brief moment of glory, being exhibited at that year's Commercial Motor Show at Earl's Court in London.

During 1949 *Commercial Motor* magazine staged a road test in Wolverhampton with a new design of Sunbeam trolleybus destined for Western Australia. Only the chassis and BTH equipment were used, with driving and observation cabs fitted to the bare frames. Wolverhampton–Bilston had been suggested for a test run, but in the event Bilston–Willenhall was selected as being more suitable, with fewer traffic problems. A top speed of 43.2mph was noted, with a balancing speed of 34mph.

On 8 May 1949 the Fighting Cocks terminus of the service to Bilston and Willenhall was moved from Dudding Road by erecting additional wiring from Parkfield Road across Dudley Road and up Goldthorn Hill to the junction of Ward Road, the wide access there allowing a turning-circle to be erected. This took pressure off the two Dudding Road bays, where inevitably congestion was experienced when vehicles on routes 8, 8A, 8B and 25 arrived out of sequence for departure. It also removed one difficult turning movement at the Dudley Road junction, although the west–south point-work was left *in situ* to allow for emergency movements and special workings. The year also saw the final phasing-out of Bell Punch and TIM ticket machines, these being replaced by the Ultimate machine, first produced by the Bell Punch Co in 1946.

On 10 October Charles Owen Silvers retired after 34 years of service as General Manager. A pioneer of trolleybus operation and an ardent supporter of the trackless principle, he is credited with being the driving force that was to transform the image of 'rail-less cars' into trolleybuses. He was succeeded by Mr R. H. Addlesee, then Deputy Manager, who was to hold this position until the end of trolleybus operation in Wolverhampton.

On 6 September a reorganisation of route numbers had been implemented with the object of removing suffixes and generally tidying up the route-numbering system. For many years it had been the practice to add an 'A' or 'B' suffix to a number for extensions to the original routes. Cross-town services had also tended to use different route numbers in each direction. The changes to trolleybus routes are shown below:

Route	Old number(s)	New number
Darlaston cross-town to Whitmore Reans via Court Road	2/7/7A	2
Darlaston cross-town to Whitmore Reans via Hordern Road	2/7/7A	7
Fordhouses cross-town to Bushbury Hill	3A/9A	3
Walsall via Willenhall (joint service)	5A	29
Wednesfield	6A	6
Bilston	7	47
Sedgley	8A	61
Dudley	8B	58
Amos Lane cross-town to Jeffcock Road	9/12	9
Low Hill cross-town to Finchfield	9B/12A	12
Low Hill cross-town to Merry Hill	9B/13	13
Penn	11A	11

Route number 29 had previously been used by a motor-bus service operating to Tong village; this was now given number 49.

The terminus of the Bilston service was altered again on 29 October, reflecting the increased requirements on the section between Bilston and Darlaston, where, at the junction with Great Bridge Road, Moxley, points were installed and additional wiring erected to a turning-circle and trolleybus lay-by, a little over 100 yards into Great Bridge Road proper, at its junction with Belmont Street. This was beneficial during peak-hour workings and was now used for most service journeys, the Fraser Street reverser only seeing use for occasional timetabled early and late workings, plus depot-access movements. Both termini continued to use route number 47.

A reduction in demand had seen short workings to/from the Courtaulds factory gradually reduced from 1946, and late in October 1949 the branch into the factory premises, reached via Hunter Street and the outbound wiring in Hordern Road, was finally taken out of use; all trolleybuses now continued down Hordern Road on route 7, turning left into Court Road past the Golden Eagle public house, and made their way back to town via Newhampton Road. The factory wires were disconnected at the Hordern Road end in November, the overhead equipment being finally removed during the summer of 1953. By the end of 1949 the unused and moribund turning-circle at Mount Road, on route 11 to Penn, had also been removed.

After much debate, prompted by a deficit of £31,054 recorded for the 1948/9 financial year, the Transport Committee had agreed a fare increase on 5 July, the first for many years. The application was put before the Traffic Commissioner, the Ministry of Transport giving approval in May 1950, with restrictions on the transfer of any monies into the General Rate Fund, it being directed that any profit should be retained in the reserve fund. Similar increases would be implemented every other year, the next being in 1952.

No new trolleybuses were purchased after 1950, the last orders featuring 99 Guy BT and Sunbeam F4 models. With success finally being achieved with the Traffic Commissioner in 1948 they were all fitted with Park Royal 8ft-wide bodywork and delivered over a period between 1948 and 1950, the last trolley to enter service being Sunbeam 630 on 2 May 1950. White steering wheels were fitted to identify the wider trolleys to drivers. This purchase allowed the withdrawal of all remaining prewar trolleybuses by 1950. The postwar designs produced different destination displays on vehicle fronts. For the first time they now used two separate roll numbers, the nearside one also containing suffix letters. The main box showed the full destination, including any 'via' information.

On 24 March 1950 nine trolleybuses were sold, for £100 each, for further service with Southend Corporation, these being four-wheel Sunbeam MF2 vehicles 264-9/71/3/5. They would have relatively short lives in their new home, the Southend system closing on 28 October 1954 and ultimately yielding Wolverhampton further supplies of traction poles and overhead equipment.

Like other municipalities, Wolverhampton was keen to mark the Golden Jubilee of its Transport Department, which fell on 1 May 1950. Two commemorative dances, with refreshments provided, were held at the Civic Hall on 2 and 9 May, and all staff were given the opportunity to attend. Officials from suppliers and nearby towns were also invited to join the festivities.

It was decided in 1951 to embark on a serious programme of rebodying, the wartime utility trolleys being the first to be dealt with. These received new bodies from Park Royal and Charles Roe, the work being spread over several batches between 1952 and 1959.

On 15 October 1951 came a change to the location of the town terminus of services 5 (Willenhall) and 29 (Walsall) with a move from the top of Horseley Fields to a new site in St James' Square, a few hundred yards further from the town centre, in an effort to avoid the growing congestion around the traffic island at the junction of Pipers Row and Horseley Fields, with its close proximity to Victoria Square. Having first negotiated the traffic island, trolleybuses had, prior to the move, loaded up for Walsall and Willenhall at the top of Horseley Fields opposite the Station Garage, adorned with the once-familiar Shell, Power and Cleveland petrol globes and owned by B. E. Hopcutt Jnr. New wiring was installed through the square, which also became the terminal point for several motor-bus services on that side of town. A small amount of redundant wiring was removed from the traffic island, the rest of the Horseley Fields wiring having to remain for depot access. At the Walsall end of the route the terminus had been moved back the previous year from the top of Park Street to Town End Bank at the back of the adjacent ABC Savoy Cinema, trolleybuses now turning a full anti-clockwise circle around the cinema to prepare for their return journey.

Above: One of 11 trolleybuses sold to Belfast Corporation in May 1952, Sunbeam MF2 294 crosses Princes Square one last time on its way to Northern Ireland. *Deryk Vernon collection*

In October/November 1951 Walsall Corporation took delivery of 10 new trolleybuses, these being Sunbeam F4 models with Brush bodywork. Numbered 334-43, they entered service on the joint route and are remembered as the most silent and smooth-running trolleybuses ever used in Walsall.

The early 1950s saw a general clearing-up of redundant sections of route, wiring being removed from the lower half of Jeffcock Road, the turning-loop at Mount Road and the reversing-triangle at Bradmore, which had been disused for many years.

In January 1952 the ex-War Department Canadian Ford towing wagon skidded in the icy weather, overturning in Sandyfields Road, Sedgley. The five crew members suffered only minor injuries, but the vehicle was less fortunate, a heavy wagon being hired in to effect recovery, while repairs to a nearby hedge cost the Transport Department £2 10s 0d.

May 1952 saw more trolleybuses sold for further service, 11 Sunbeam MF2s (282/6-95) passing to Belfast Corporation for £150 each. By the end of the year 16 of the 7ft 6in-wide trolleybuses (402-17) had been rebodied. Fitted with a distinctive and dated (though not unattractive) style of bodywork by Park Royal, they became known as the '402' class; all save 408, which had carried a Weymann utility body, had previously been fitted with Park Royal utility bodywork. During the summer Bilston depot's turntable received attention, being given a full overhaul by the Department's mechanical staff.

On 10 January 1955 the Wednesfield route (6) was extended down Lichfield Road towards Bloxwich as far as the turn for Linthouse Lane, opposite the Albion Hotel, built in the early 1950s and standing on the corner of Stubby Lane. The service to Wednesfield had become increasingly busy and from March 1954 had been strengthened by weekday peak-hour motor-bus workings on new route 1; these were withdrawn when the trolleybus route was extended. The extension was intended to serve an overspill estate of 2,350 houses and was constructed at a cost of £663 using traction poles and bracket arms purchased from Birmingham City Transport's ex-tramway stock. Allocated route number 59 and terminating at Wednesfield (The Albion), it first ran alternately with route 6, which still showed the destination as Wood End. Service 6 was eventually withdrawn from 7 September 1959 in favour of an increased 59 service. The turning-circle in High Street was left *in situ* until final abandonment of the Wednesfield route in 1963.

One improvement in 1955 was the introduction of a short-wave radio system, enabling tower-wagon crews and inspectors to be directed more rapidly to breakdowns and accidents, thereby keeping disruption to a minimum. In December the Transport Committee reviewed the future of the trolleybus system yet again, looking at the minutes of previous meetings in 1939/40 and March 1945. Again it was decided not to change the overall policy and to continue to retain the system.

In February 1956 a fire saw the North Street end of Queen Square closed to traffic as the Hippodrome (opened in 1898 as the Empire Palace of Varieties) took light. Power was cut to the overhead wiring in Queen Square, to assist firemen who fought for many hours to contain the fire.

A further extension, the last on the trolleybus system, opened on 25 June 1956 and took route 9 beyond the Amos Lane reverser 600 yards down Prestwood Road to a new housing estate on the edge of Ashmore Park, making use of a traffic island outside The Pheasant public house at the junction with Wood End Road. The new service was inaugurated by trolleybus 475, a Sunbeam F4, at 9.10am. An extension to link up with the terminus of service 6 at the other end of Wood End Road was often considered but never put into practice. The reversing triangle at the old terminus was removed, but the destination blinds continued to show Amos Lane until closure of the trolleybus route.

In 1957 the first signs of forthcoming problems began to loom on the horizon. Several trolleybus operators, including Wolverhampton Corporation, approached the Government of the day with a request that the restrictions then in place covering operation and expansion be lifted or, at the very least, eased. The request was to some extent prompted by the aftermath of the fuel situation in 1956 following a strangling of supplies, caused by the Suez crisis. London had already decided on a policy of trolleybus abandonment, and in the light of this decision the Government took the somewhat short-sighted decision to refuse the request. The system was now operating at its maximum, and it was concluded that any future needs with regard to trolleybus operation (or not) would be decided on the merits of each case as the requirement arose.

A report from the General Manager, presented in June 1957, implied that 99 of Wolverhampton's 153 trolleybuses were in need of some form of replacement. As an interim measure the Committee agreed to the upgrading and rebodying of the chassis of the utility trolleybuses and the replacement of the Park Lane substation with extramway equipment purchased from Leeds City Transport. Nationalisation had also arrived in the form of the electricity supply, the Corporation now buying in its requirements rather than using its own generating station, which in turn had increased electricity costs. Varied opinions were put forward regarding retention or scrapping of the system, including cost differentials with new motor buses and the high costs and disruption involved in extending trolleybus routes to new housing estates. One casualty of this somewhat short-sighted view was the axing of the proposed extension of route 9 along Linthouse Lane to link up with routes 6 and 59, which potentially useful circular service was never to see the light of day.

On 13 April 1959 trolleybus 630 was involved in a serious accident on a routine trip to Penn Fields. A lorry from Cleveland Street crossed a set of traffic lights at red, causing the trolleybus to swerve out of control in Worcester Street and ram a shop front. So deeply embedded was 630 that the upper floor of the building had to be supported with jacks while the trolleybus was gently extracted. It was a delicate task with very little clearance between the jacks and the sides of the vehicle.

During the late 1950s and early 1960s, to streamline operations, a number of tidying-up alterations were made to the town-centre overhead layouts. The outbound points in Chapel Ash, separating the Tettenhall and Bradmore routes, were moved back to the bottom of Darlington Street, close to the old horse tram depot, with electric point operation installed. Similarly the outbound points in Queen Square were moved back some distance into Lichfield Street, allowing Victoria Street trolleys to leapfrog the loading points for Chapel Ash-bound vehicles, a diamond crossing at the entrance to Queen Square allowing the process to be reversed as services 4, 9, 11 and 32 loaded up with homeward-bound passengers. In the reverse direction another diamond crossing at the top of Queen Square allowed inbound trolleys from Victoria Street to pass services 1, 12 and 13 as they unloaded, in turn passing services 4, 9, 11 and 32 as they discharged their passengers outside the Art Gallery in Lichfield Street. Out in the suburbs the loading point on route 9 for inbound journeys was moved from outside the shops in busy Jeffcock Road and around the corner into the quieter but narrower Rayleigh Road. The destination blinds were left unaltered as 'JEFFCOCK ROAD VIA GREAT BRICKKILN STREET', as the unloading point remained in Jeffcock Road, just past the reverser in Downham Place.

More updating of the fleet took place between 1958 and 1962, 38 utility trollies receiving a new and more modern style of body from Charles H. Roe of Leeds, the total cost of these being £114,000. This now left the Corporation with a fleet consisting of three basic types of trolleybus, to wit:

402-17	Sunbeam/Park Royal rebodied vehicles ('402' class)
418-55	Sunbeam/Roe rebodied vehicles
456-654	Sunbeam or Guy/Park Royal 8ft-wide body

Of the third group, it should be noted that 482-607 and 631-54 were, according to the order book, of Guy manufacture, but there was little externally to distinguish this, other than the absence of Sunbeam's triangular badge on the front of the driver's cab.

During the penultimate month of 1959 an experimental dark-green livery was applied to trolleybuses 409/12/71/90, 603/53, as well as to some motor buses. This livery, it was claimed, was reflective in the dark and gave extra safety protection, although the end result, which was relieved by a narrow straw-coloured waist band, was not universally liked by the public, nor did it wear well or appear to be particularly effective. Most of the trolleys were eventually repainted in the standard fleet livery, with the exception of 471, which was to retain the experimental colour until July 1963, and 653, left to soldier on alone and end its days in the non-standard livery.

Illuminated semaphore-arm indicators were to disappear in 1960, as replacement flashing units were fitted to all trolleybuses. There was somewhat of a precedent for this, as the anomalous position in law still allowed the trolleybus some privileges not given to others, and, although in the early 1950s anything except semaphore indicators would have been illegal for other traffic, there was nothing to stop Bradford trolleybus 758 becoming the first vehicle to use flashing indicators lawfully. In 1959 raised shrouds set over the trolleybase were still fitted to a number of FJW-registered trolleys, although most of these would be removed over the next two years. Park Royal-bodied Sunbeam 458 was the odd man out, retaining both its semaphore arms and trolleybase covers until withdrawal on New Year's Eve 1961.

During 1959 the Walsall Sunbeam F4 trolleybuses operating on joint route 29 were displaced to local workings by the entry into service of eight second-hand Sunbeam W models purchased from Hastings Tramways, the interiors still painted in the style of their previous owner. Fitted with 56-seat Weymann bodywork, Nos 303-10 were never popular with either crews or passengers, having a neglected look and cramped layout, but could put on a surprisingly good turn of speed and were placed straight into service on the busy Wolverhampton route.

On 12 September 1960 both trolleybus and motor-bus services were stopped during the day while the freedom of the town was given to the former North Staffordshire and South Staffordshire regiments by Wolverhampton County Borough Council. A full march-past took place through the town centre with a military band playing and the soldiers marching with fixed bayonets.

A general fare increase was applied with effect from 29 September. Most ordinary fares between 3d and 6½d were increased by ½d, concessionary fares between 6½d

Above: Guy BT 600 at Downham Place, with the driver being trained in the skilled art of using a reverser. Note the window-cleaner's handcart parked next to the kerb. *John Hughes collection*

and 11d being withdrawn. Those of 1s 4d or more were increased by 2d. The year was also to see an end to the regular use of Lower Stafford Street for diversions on route 3 to Fordhouses, whereby North Street used to be briefly closed at the end of football matches. The wiring, however, remained in place, live and still connected at each end by pointwork, until the end of trolleybus operation on the cross-town service between Fordhouses and Bushbury Hill.

At the start of the 1950s motor buses had accounted for just over one third of the combined Wolverhampton fleet; 10 years later this had risen to just short of 50% with 149 buses, against 153 trolleybuses. Nevertheless the number of passengers travelling by trolleybus had continued to rise, reaching a peak in 1960, and the decade had seen a considerable increase in activity at Cleveland Road depot as further routes and vehicles were added to the system, leading to a growth in the associated wiring. That outside the depot was notorious for its complexity, the up and down wires from Snow Hill, Transport Road and Bilston Road merging into one pair as the depot frontage was reached. Wiring into the depot branched off in both directions outside each entrance bay. Forward and reverse direction for the trolleybuses was covered by the master controller in the driver's cab, with reversed field windings in the controller ensuring that continuity of direction was maintained as the trolley booms switched to wires with a different polarity. However, drivers had to be visually aware when moving across the section breaks and avoid drawing current. The dexterity required on the power pedal as a result produced many a budding Fred Astaire, and any failure on the part of the driver to observe these precautions would result in arcing across the dead section, producing a burnt insulator with damage sustained to wire surface and the likely tripping-out of the circuit-breakers in the cab roof. The section outside the workshop bay and car shed was particularly testing, with a crossover, plus up and down wiring merging, all within a few yards. Leaving the depot was also potentially hazardous: from the very beginning trolleybuses taking up service had, with few exceptions, reversed out of the depot and into the centre of the road — a practice which, despite criticisms from official sources on the grounds of safety and visibility, would persist until the very end.

Right: Willenhall. Having arrived on route 5, Guy BT 483 heads two other trolleys bound for Walsall. Both the other vehicles are Walsall Corporation trolleys, being 308, an ex-Hastings Sunbeam W with Weymann bodywork and an unidentified 30ft-long Sunbeam F4A with Willowbrook bodywork. *John Hughes collection*

Above: Sunbeam W4 412 in Bilston, turning out of Mount Pleasant into Lichfield Street and displaying an incorrect Fighting Cocks (Dudding Road) destination. The trolleybus is in the experimental dark green livery. *John Hughes collection*

Above: Guy BT trolleybuses 603 and 653, in the experimental dark-green livery, share the busy Fighting Cocks bays with a sister trolley and mobile tea van as a fourth trolley speeds past on its way to Dudley. *Deryk Vernon collection*

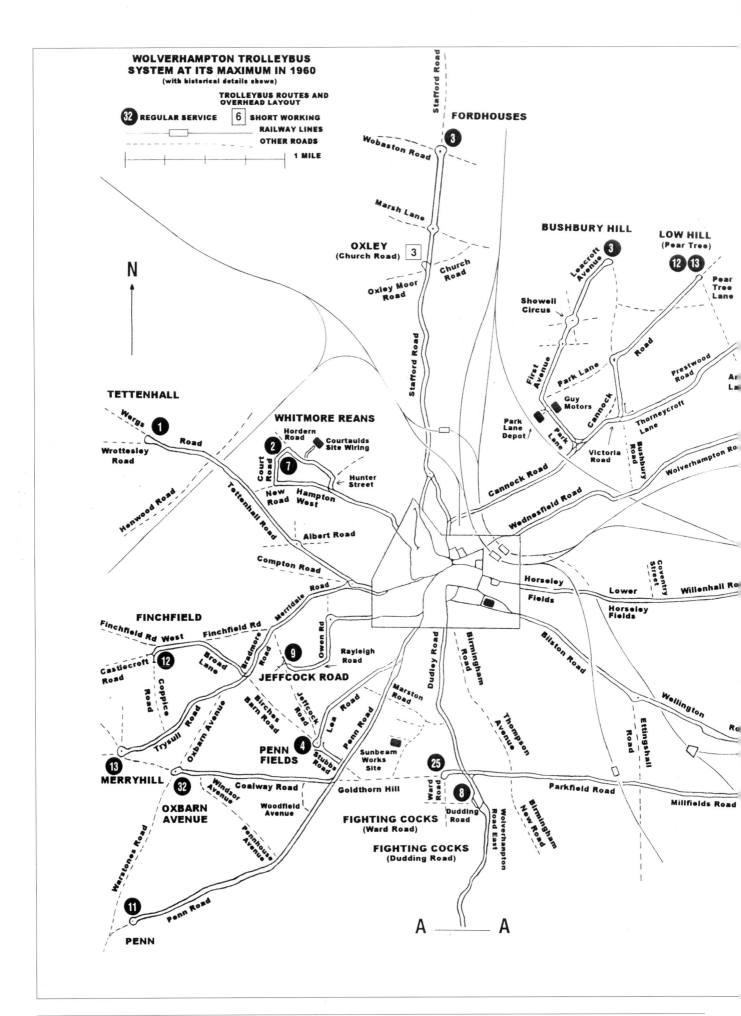

WOLVERHAMPTON TROLLEYBUS
SYSTEM AT ITS MAXIMUM IN 1960
(with historical details shown)

TROLLEYBUS ROUTES AND OVERHEAD LAYOUT

32 REGULAR SERVICE   **6** SHORT WORKING

RAILWAY LINES

OTHER ROADS

1 MILE

N

FORDHOUSES

Stafford Road

Wobaston Road

Marsh Lane

3

OXLEY
(Church Road)

3

Oxley Moor Road

Church Road

Stafford Road

BUSHBURY HILL

LOW HILL
(Pear Tree)

12 **13**

Leacroft Avenue

Showell Circus

First Avenue

Park Lane

Cannock Road

Pear Tree Lane

Prestwood Road

Thorneycroft Lane

Guy Motors

Park Lane Depot

Park Lane

Victoria Road

Bushbury Road

Wolverhampton Ro

3

Cannock Road

Wednesfield Road

TETTENHALL

Wergs Road

Wrottesley Road

Henwood Road

Tettenhall Road

WHITMORE REANS

Hordern Road

Court Road

Courtaulds Site Wiring

2

7

Hunter Street

New Road

Hampton West

Albert Road

Compton Road

Road

Horseley Fields

Lower Horseley Fields

Coventry Street

Willenhall Ro

FINCHFIELD

Finchfield Rd West

Finchfield Rd

Merridale Road

Bradmore Road

Owen Rd

Rayleigh Road

Bilston Road

12

Castlecroft Road

Coppice Road

Broad Lane

Birches Barn Road

Jeffcock Road

9

JEFFCOCK ROAD

Lea Road

Penn Road

Marston Road

Dudley Road

Birmingham Road

Thompson Avenue

Wellington Ro

Ettingshall Road

Trysull Road

Oxbarn Avenue

Stubbs Road

4

PENN FIELDS

Sunbeam Works Site

25

Parkfield Road

Millfields Road

13

32

MERRYHILL

Windsor Avenue

Coalway Road

Woodfield Avenue

Goldthorn Hill

Ward Road

8

Dudding Road

Wolverhampton Road East

Birmingham New Road

OXBARN AVENUE

Pennhouse Avenue

FIGHTING COCKS
(Ward Road)

Warstones Road

FIGHTING COCKS
(Dudding Road)

11

Penn Road

A ——— A

PENN

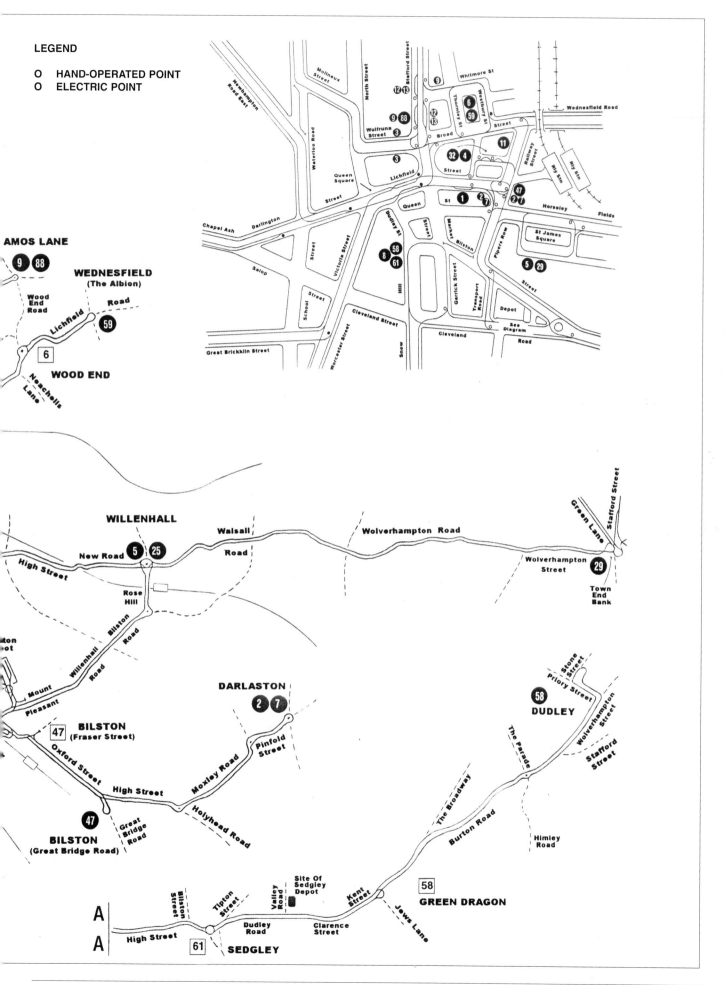

LEGEND

O   HAND-OPERATED POINT
O   ELECTRIC POINT

Left: A sunny interlude on Tuesday 26 September 1961 as Guy BT 601 waits in the Victoria Square loop before moving up Lichfield Street to the loading point outside the General Post Office. *John Hughes collection*

Right: Sunbeam F4 614 waits at the loading point outside the General Post Office in Lichfield Street, with its booms safely tucked into the overhead parking loop. The Grand Theatre and Preedy's tobacconists can be seen further down the street. *John Hughes collection*

Left: Sunbeam F4 624 comes down through Queen Square towards Darlington Street on an outbound working on Friday 1 September 1961. The trolley is about to cross the wiring from Victoria Street, as a 'Bobby' on traffic duty holds back oncoming traffic. *John Hughes collection*

Left: A busy scene in Chapel Ash. Guy BT 651 passes Lovatt Street as it travels towards Darlington Street and the town centre, while in the distance can be seen an outbound trolleybus under the Tettenhall wires; the adjacent wiring will peel off into Merridale Road to serve routes 12 and 13 to Finchfield and Merry Hill respectively. *John Hughes collection*

Right: Sunbeam F4 626 climbs steadily up through The Rock in dappled sunlight as it nears the terminus at Upper Green on 10 September 1962. *John Hughes collection*

Left: An idyllic moment in the sunshine at Tettenhall Green as the crew of Sunbeam F4 624 relax before returning to town. The waiting shelter behind the trolleybus had seen many years of service, having been used originally at the 1902 Wolverhampton Arts & Industrial Exhibition held in West Park. It saw trams, trolleybuses and Corporation motor buses come and go, finally succumbing in 1972. *John Hughes collection*

Routes 2, 7 and 47:
Whitmore Reans–Wolverhampton–Bilston–Darlaston

Left: Sunbeam F4 608 sits at the Court Road terminus of route 7 in 1950. Beyond Hordern Road can be seen one of the four Courtaulds Works chimneys, with another looming over the rooftops behind 608. Courtaulds, an American-owned company making viscose yarn, set up its Wolverhampton premises in 1916. A short extension off route 7 was laid into the works from Hordern Road, lasting until 1949. *Author's collection*

Right: A sun shower leaves the road surface glistening on a bright Saturday afternoon in June 1964, as Guy BT 654 departs from the Whitmore Reans terminus of route 7 in Court Road on a journey that will take it across town to Bilston and Darlaston. *Author*

Left: Guy BT 646 edges past the Guy Warrior tower wagon on maintenance work as it negotiates the turn from Hunter Street into Coleman Street. After a short distance it will turn into Hordern Road for the run down to the terminus in Court Road. *John Hughes collection*

Left: Newhampton Road West in 1962. On an outbound working on route 7 to Whitmore Reans Guy BT 649 turns into Hunter Street past the local branch of Timothy Whites chemist, another name that has sadly disappeared from our streets. Note, at the top of the picture, the overhead skate for operating the electric points; the indicator box is attached to the traction pole above the two pedestrians. The terraced houses on the right of Newhampton Road have largely disappeared through redevelopment. *Author*

Right: Newhampton Road West. Heading for Whitmore Reans, 476 swings into Hunter Street at the divergence point of routes 2 and 7. This was also the line taken by trolleybuses operating into the Courtaulds works, though they used route number 2. *Author*

Left: Sunbeam F4 633 makes its way along Lichfield Street *en route* for Whitmore Reans via Hordern Road. Parked in the loop outside the General Post Office is sister trolley 614, which will shortly set off for Tettenhall. Further down Lichfield Street can be seen the Grand Theatre; designed by C. J. Phipps, an experienced theatre architect, this had opened on 10 December 1894. *John Hughes collection*

Left: Park Royal-bodied 409, a Sunbeam W4, waits in Victoria Square before setting off for Bilston and Darlaston. The absence of traffic and the closed shops suggest this is a Sunday working. *John Hughes collection*

Right: Victoria Square. On a chilly winter's day in February 1964 Sunbeam utility No 403 stands with a sister vehicle while waiting to depart for Bilston and Darlaston. The second trolley is on route 47 (which operated Mon-Sat only) and will work to Bilston (Great Bridge Road). *Author*

Left: Guy BT 648 speeds along Bilston Road near Culwick Street on a wet and miserable day in 1962. Note the interesting combination of span wires, bracket arms and pull-off wires. The fence on the right is virtually at the point where today's Midland Metro tram system leaves the main road and descends the embankment to use the trackbed of the old Great Western Railway main line to Birmingham.
John Hughes collection

Left: An 8ft-wide Sunbeam approaches Bilston town centre along Wellington Road. Note the electric milk-float and the articulated log lorry in this early-postwar scene. *John Hughes collection*

Right: Guy BT 492 loads up at the top of Oxford Street in Bilston before proceeding to Darlaston. Fraser Street and its associated reverser are immediately behind. The poster on the wall is advertising tickets to see Marty Wilde at the local Gaumont cinema. *John Hughes collection*

Left: Roe-bodied Sunbeam 451 backs into Fraser Street on the reversing triangle prior to returning to Wolverhampton, much to the consternation of a Volkswagen driver trying to reach Oxford Street! Confusingly, the destination reads 'Whitmore Reans'. The loading point for Darlaston-bound trolleys can be seen to the right. *John Hughes collection*

Left: Fraser Street reverser. A small boy watches intently as Sunbeam F4 468 backs around the corner. It has just come from Bilston depot and is using the reverser to gain the wiring to Wolverhampton, where it will enter service on route 2. *Author*

Right: Roe-bodied Sunbeam W4 sisters 442 and 441 gleam in the sun as they pause at the Oxford Street loading stop in Bilston, on their way to Darlaston and Great Bridge Road, in June 1964. Fraser Street reverser can be seen behind 441. *Author*

Left: A busy scene in Oxford Street as Guy BT 646 on route 47 waits to turn into Great Bridge Road while 443 and another Roe-bodied trolley pass on the Whitmore Reans–Darlaston through service. *Author*

Left: On a Saturday evening in late August 1965, with the sun glinting across the camera lens, Sunbeam W4 utility 408 coasts under the pointwork and across Great Bridge Road junction on an inbound journey from Darlaston to Wolverhampton and Whitmore Reans. *Author*

Right: **Moxley, 1965.** A Sunbeam utility swings out of Moxley Road into High Street on its way back to Wolverhampton. *Author*

Left: Sunbeam/Roe 453 keeps an elderly '402'-class utility company at the unloading stop in Pinfold Street, Darlaston, outside the Wesleyan Chapel (seen on the right of the picture) and just short of the turning-circle at the Bull Stake. *John Hughes collection*

Above: Fordhouses terminus, with The Vine public house dominating the view next to the traffic island. Sunbeam W4 utility 405 waits for the 'right time' before departing on the journey across town to Bushbury Hill. *John Hughes collection*

Above: Sunbeam 440 at the little-used Oxley (Church Road) short-working terminus on 28 March 1961. Church Road was actually on the other side of Stafford Road, the turning loop being in the entrance to Oxley Moor Road. *John Hughes collection*

Left: Trolley 445 descends North Street past the Wolverhampton Wanderers football ground on a murky Saturday afternoon in January 1964, shortly before abandonment of the route. Another trolleybus breasts the hill into town as the tower of St Peter's collegiate church rises ghost-like on the skyline. North Street was to disappear under redevelopment and an extension of the Wolves ground. *Author*

Left: Wulfruna Street. Sunbeam F4 465 waits outside the Technical College to depart to Bushbury Hill. The fur coats that found popularity with the ladies in the 1960s are much in evidence. *John Hughes collection*

Left: Sunbeam 470 passes Dennis Taylor's chemist shop on the corner of Charles Street as it heads down Stafford Street on its way out of town to Bushbury Hill in 1961. In the distance can be seen another trolleybus waiting to leave for either Finchfield or Merryhill. *John Hughes collection*

Left: Having just turned left out of Cannock Road by the Elephant & Castle public house, Park Royal-bodied Sunbeam F4 473 starts the climb up Stafford Street on the last leg of its journey into town. In the distance can be seen the wiring in Lower Stafford Street. *John Hughes collection*

Left: Looking remarkably like one of its 7ft 6in-wide utility cousins, trolleybus 465, an 8ft-wide Sunbeam F4, toils up the hill to swing left out of Cannock Road into Stafford Street. Up on the bridge a British Rail Class 08 diesel shunter moves wagons into the ex-GWR Herbert Street goods depot. *John Hughes collection*

Right: Early evening in Bushbury on Sunday 21 January 1964, the last day of trolleybus operation, as Sunbeam/Roe 446 rounds the island at Showell Circus, its interior lights already on to cope with the encroaching gloom, as the trolleybus passes the blue-painted Police telephone box on the corner. *Author*

Above: **Sunbeam W4 trolleys 455 and 445 pass at the terminus near the top of Bushbury Hill. Beyond lay a sloping panorama of semi-open countryside.** *John Hughes collection*

Above: **The summit of Bushbury Hill, with 8ft-wide Sunbeam F4 473 parked under the trees at the top of the turning-circle.**
John Hughes collection

Route 4: Wolverhampton–Penn Fields

Left: In company with an Austin A40, Guy BT 650 stands in bright sunshine at the Chubb Street terminus alongside the famous lock works established by Charles and Jeremiah Chubb in 1818. The front wheel has been chocked, the crew being at the nearby Railway Street staff canteen, while the trolley booms are still on the through wires, suggesting that the photograph was taken after the closure of route 32. Behind can be seen the rear of the Co-Operative Emporium in Short Street, the frontage being in Lichfield Street opposite the Grand Theatre. *John Hughes collection*

Right: Its driver holding back the handbrake to control his descent to Chubb Street, Guy BT 624 swings into Fryer Street, past the Sir Tatton Sykes public house. Behind 624, on the far side of Victoria Square, can be seen the Victoria Hotel, while in the centre of the square, taxis wait beneath the clock. *John Hughes collection*

Left: Guy BT 603 swings across the traffic at the junction of Lea Road and Penn Road to continue its journey down Lea Road as another trolley turns into Penn Road on its way back to town. One car driver seems determined to beat the town-bound trolley, at any risk to himself. *John Hughes collection*

Left: Having unloaded at Penn Fields terminus, Guy BT 497 moves up to the traffic island and, circling it, will draw up by the queue of people waiting on the far side at the bus stop under the trees. A tower wagon is busy with remedial work on the tie-off point for the Stubbs Road emergency wiring, just visible on the right of the picture. *John Hughes collection*

Left: Roe-bodied Sunbeam W4 426 waits under the trees at Lea Road terminus. Note the 'BUS FOR TOWN' legend on the bus stop. The traffic island around which 426 has just turned can be seen in the background. *John Hughes collection*

Routes 5 and 29: Wolverhampton–Willenhall–Walsall

Right: St James Square. Guy BT 654 speeds away from the loading bays at the start of its journey to Willenhall and Walsall. This trolleybus was destined to operate the final tour on Sunday 5 March 1967 in company with Rotherham 44, prior to a less-than-glorious life and sad decline in the supposedly safe hands of preservationists. *John Hughes collection*

Left: Horseley Fields 1965. The morning light catches Sunbeam 465 as it turns into St James's Square on wiring normally used for access to and from Cleveland Road depot. The trolley will take up duties on route 5, its destination blind having already been set for Willenhall. *Author*

Right: Walsall 346, an ex-Ipswich Sunbeam F4 with Park Royal bodywork, is seen entering St James's Square in 1965, having arrived from Walsall on the jointly operated route 29. *Author*

Right: In another 1965 scene Walsall 341, a Sunbeam F4 with a Brush body, new in 1951, waits to leave St James Square for Walsall. The presence behind of an 8ft-wide Wolverhampton trolley suggests that the next few trolleys on this route would all be Wolverhampton Corporation vehicles, the two towns always operating their respective fleets in convoy. *Author*

Left: St James Square in 1965. Guy BT 654 and Sunbeam W4 434 head a line of trolleys waiting to load up. The last day of trolleybus operation in Wolverhampton would see 654, freshly repainted, touring the remaining route to Dudley in company with Rotherham 44 — a swansong performance for both vehicles. *Author*

Left: A very rare photograph of a Walsall Corporation trolleybus, in this instance Sunbeam F4 345, purchased second-hand from Ipswich in 1962, alongside Guy BT 603, one of the six trolleybuses to carry the experimental dark-green livery, applied in November 1959. The location is St James Square, Wolverhampton. *Author's collection*

Above: Walsall and Wolverhampton trolleys pass underneath the Lower Horseley Fields railway bridge. *Author*

Above: With the Midland Bank on the corner of Market Place as a backdrop, Sunbeam 429 swings around the traffic island in the centre of Willenhall to collect its queue of Wolverhampton-bound passengers. The destination blind has not yet been altered to read 'WOLVERHAMPTON' and still displays 'WILLENHALL'. *John Hughes collection*

Left: The driver of Wolverhampton-bound Guy BT 605 slows on his way across the Willenhall traffic island to allow his 'clippie' to sprint to a nearby traction pole and pull the cord for the manually controlled pointwork, allowing the trolley booms to take the Wolverhampton wires. *John Hughes collection*

Left: Sunbeam 420 stands at the Willenhall terminus in New Road, sharing the parking bay with Walsall 352, an ex-Ipswich vehicle. The blue trolley will continue to Walsall on the jointly operated route 29. *Author*

Left: As a Hillman Imp car heads for Walsall town centre a Roe-bodied trolleybus emerges from the side street behind the ABC Savoy cinema at Townend Bank to commence its journey home. *John Hughes collection*

Routes 6 and 59: Wolverhampton–Wood End–Wednesfield

Right: Sunbeam W4 utility 405 stands in Thornley Street with another trolleybus while the crew take a break before setting off for Wednesfield. *John Hughes collection*

Right: Sunbeam F4 471 waits in Thornley Street. This was one of the six trolleybuses repainted in an experimental dark-green livery. *Author's collection*

Left: Coming up Broad Street with the High Level railway visible in the distance, Sunbeam F4 470 prepares to turn right into Thornley Street and discharge its passengers. Note the array of period bicycles outside the sweet shop. *John Hughes collection*

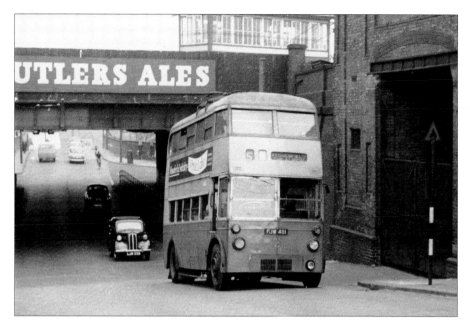

Left: With the High Level station signalbox above, Sunbeam 481 makes the short climb over Broad Street canal bridge, the old canal warehouse entrance being adjacent to the trolleybus. Just beyond the bridge can be seen the turn down to Wolverhampton's ex-Great Western Low Level railway station, with the overbridge behind the cyclist. *John Hughes collection*

Right: Heading into town, Guy BT 497 breasts the steep climb over Broad Street canal bridge at its junction with Railway Street. A train can be seen crossing the railway bridge as it enters the High Level station. The canal bridge was removed during construction of the inner ring road and has now been re-erected at the Black Country Living Museum, appropriately within a few feet of the operating trolleybus system, although sadly they are not yet routed over the bridge. *Author's collection*

Left: On the turning-loop at Linthouse Lane, Sunbeam F4 465 swings across Lichfield Road towards The Albion public house (after which the terminus was named) before starting its run back to town. *John Hughes collection*

Routes 8, 58 and 61:
Wolverhampton–Fighting Cocks–Sedgley–Dudley

Right: Park Royal-bodied Sunbeam W4 408 stands at the unloading point in town at the top of Bell Street, with Atkinson's Coach & Horses public house on the corner. *Author's collection*

Left: A deserted Bilston Street in May 1964. It is 9.30pm and the rain has just stopped as Roe-bodied Sunbeam W4 451 waits patiently for passengers. This trolleybus was one of a select group that would survive to the end of the system, appearing at this location on Sunday 5 March 1967. *Author*

Left: Roe-bodied Sunbeam W4 423 leads a utility and an 8ft-wide Park Royal-bodied trolley at the Dudley loading stop in Bilston Street in June 1964. *Author*

Above: Sunbeam W4 436 rounds the corner from Bilston Street into Garrick Street as it departs for the run to Fighting Cocks. Towering above the trolleybus is the spire of nearby Queen Street Congregational Church, designed by architect George Bidlake and built 1864-6. *John Hughes collection*

Left: Running repairs in Garrick Street. A Roe-bodied trolley eases past a tower wagon parked in front of local opticians, Scrivens, as it departs on the six-mile run to Dudley. Despite the enticement of Jack Green's well-stocked bicycle shop (next to the opticians) many people have brought their cars into town, parking them on the waste ground to the left of the trolley, where a terrace of small shops and homes has been cleared in anticipation of redevelopment. The site of today's Midland Metro tram terminus is just out of the picture, to the right of Jack Green's shop. *Author*

Right: Snow Hill-bound, Park Royal-bodied Sunbeam F4 626 crosses route 25 at Fighting Cocks on 11 April 1965. *John Hughes collection*

Left: A timeless scene featuring three trolleys at the Dudding Road terminus. Preparing to leave for Wolverhampton via the through bay wiring, Sunbeam W4 413 was unique in having a flush-fitting sliding cab door. Meanwhile two more trolleys, led by Guy BT 643, stand in the bay used by vehicles on route 8. *John Hughes collection*

Opposite: An unusual view of 602 awaiting 'right time' departure at Fighting Cocks. *John Hughes collection*

Left: In driving rain two trolleys make their way across the traffic lights at Parkfield Road, outside the Fighting Cocks public house, as they head back to town. *Author*

Right: Accelerating away from Fighting Cocks towards Sedgley, Sunbeam 451 clears the pointwork as another Roe-bodied trolley leaves the through bay on a return trip to town. *John Hughes collection*

Left: The rain has just abated as Sunbeam W4 utility 416 climbs Wolverhampton Road at the start of the long haul up to Sedgley in July 1964. *Author*

Left: The hill between Fighting Cocks and Sedgley on a Sunday morning in 1965. The overhead-maintenance crew deal with a failed wiring spacer as a utility trolley returning from Dudley creeps past the problem area. *Author*

Right: In the high summer of 1965 Saturday shuttle workings were often instituted between Dudley and Sedgley, using route number 61, to cope with the crowds of people wishing to travel, the full loop of wiring at Sedgley proving very useful. Sunbeam 440 is seen manœuvring around the Bull Ring as it prepares to return to Dudley; also visible, parked alongside the Clifton cinema, is a Midland Red single-deck bus waiting to depart on a local journey. *Author*

Left: Roe-bodied Sunbeam W4 trolleys 441 and 455 bask in the bright sunshine at the loading points in Dudley Street, Sedgley, June 1965. *Author*

Routes 9 and 88:
Jeffcock Road–Wolverhampton–Amos Lane

Left: Roe-bodied Sunbeam W4 422 unloads at the terminus in Jeffcock Road, literally at the end of the line. Many years previously the wiring had continued down Jeffcock Road, running through to Bradmore and Finchfield. *Author's collection*

Right: A pleasant sunny morning in Rayleigh Road, with Jeffcock Road in the background. No 464, a Sunbeam F4, will shortly depart with the cross-town service to Amos Lane. The white coloured steering wheel, used to indicate an 8ft-wide trolley, is quite conspicuous in the driver's cab. *John Hughes collection*

Left: Worcester Street. Sunbeam W4 445 turns into Great Brickkiln Street as it leaves town for Jeffcock Road. The Studio Bannerjee shop, where you could have your hand-tinted black-and-white photographic portrait taken, can be seen on the left corner. *John Hughes collection*

Left: SunbeamW4/Roe 421 swings across Princes Square into Lichfield Street past a bobby on traffic duty as it heads out of town. The policeman is standing next to the country's first set of permanently installed traffic lights (October 1928) complete with the well-known blue 'TURNING RIGHT – KEEP RIGHT' signs. *John Hughes collection*

Right: Utility Sunbeam W4 trolley 402 turns right into Cannock Road from Stafford Street. The wiring in the foreground is for Lower Stafford Street; retained for emergencies and football-game diversions from North Street, it saw little use towards the end. *John Hughes collection*

Left: With The Pheasant public house and turning-circle in the background Sunbeam W4 447, still with its original Park Royal utility body, waits at the terminus before heading back to town and Jeffcock Road. Although the route was extended to this point in 1956, the destination blinds continued to read 'AMOS LANE VIA FALLINGS PARK'. *John Hughes collection*

Route 11: Wolverhampton–Penn

Left: A quiet moment in Railway Street as Guy BT 489 waits with handbrake firmly on and front wheel chocked against the gradient, the open cab door indicating that the crew are probably in the nearby canteen. In the distance the wiring for routes 4 and 32 can be seen emerging from Chubb Street. *John Hughes collection*

Left: Princes Square. Closely followed by another trolleybus, Sunbeam W 411 exits from Broad Street to swing right into Lichfield Street. *John Hughes collection*

Right: A motorcycle — possibly a Velocette — with L-plates fitted passes a Morris Minor car complete with early-pattern split windscreen as Guy BT 493 follows out of Princes Square into Lichfield Street.
John Hughes collection

Left: Penn Road between Coalway Road and Mount Road. Sunbeam W4 414 drops off a passenger at the Coalway Avenue stop. Note the absence of other traffic on what is now the busy A449 to Kidderminster and Worcester. *John Hughes collection*

Left: Guy BT 499 leads a Swindon-bound motor bus across the traffic lights at the junction of Penn Road with Stubbs Road. *Author's collection*

Right: A beautiful period photograph taken *c*1952 at Penn terminus, as Sunbeam W4 447 loads up before travelling back to town. Note the elderly St Ivel cheese van unloading at the shops while the trolleybus crew stretch their legs and chat at the bus stop. Fitted with a 54-seat Park Royal body, this trolleybus entered service on 23 December 1947 and would rebodied by Roe with a 60-seat body in April 1961. The scene has now changed somewhat but is still quite recognisable: the housing has been extended down to the shops, which are still in evidence and much as seen, but the road has now become a busy dual carriageway. *John Hughes collection*

Routes 12 and 13:
Finchfield/Merry Hill–Wolverhampton–Low Hill

Left: Sunbeam/Roe 436 stands at the Merry Hill terminus on a damp and misty day. A delivery from the nationally known and locally based Mander's paint company can be seen in the pub car park. *John Hughes collection*

Right: Having cleared the points for route 12 at Broad Lane, a Park Royal-bodied trolley travels through Bradmore past the local Star Stores on its way down Trysull Road to Merry Hill terminus. Notice the family group; the little boy is wearing what appears to be a regulation school uniform, complete with cap. The photograph was taken c1960. *John Hughes collection*

Left: On arrival at Finchfield terminus Sunbeam F4 456 has turned into Coppice Road using the reverser and will now back into Castlecroft Road towards the white-painted drainpipes on the left of the picture. *Author's collection*

Right: Having reversed into Castlecroft Road, Sunbeam utility 403 draws forward past the New Inn public house to cross to the nearside of Finchfield Road West. *Author's collection*

Left: Sunbeam/Roe 423 pictured at the loading-point in 1960. Note, on the left of the picture, the unloading stop and the reverser into Coppice Road. *John Hughes collection*

Right: Broad Lane, bordering the expanse of Bantock Park, appears quite rural as Sunbeam W4 utility 417 heads towards Bradmore and the town centre. Bantock House and its substantial grounds were donated to the town by Mrs Bantock on 13 June 1938, shortly after the death of her husband, Alderman Albert Baldwin Bantock, the Council gratefully accepting this gift and deciding that the land should become a public park. The house is open to the public, the contents forming a local museum. *Author's collection*

Above: Still in the experimental dark-green livery, Finchfield-bound Sunbeam F4 471 leads a convoy of trolleybuses, including sister vehicle 470, through Princes Square in 1961. *John Hughes collection*

Right: Sunbeams 441 and 463, with contrasting styles of bodywork by Roe and Park Royal, stand in the loading-loop at the top of Stafford Street prior to departure for Merry Hill and Finchfield respectively. *John Hughes collection*

Left: Sunbeam utility 403 waits in Stafford Street before continuing its cross-town working to Low Hill (Pear Tree) on route 13. Behind 403 can be seen a Roe-bodied W4 on an Amos Lane working, as can the overhead-line parking loops that were a well-used feature of town-centre wiring in Wolverhampton. *Author*

Above: Cannock Road in 1963. Bound for Low Hill, Guy BT 607 draws up to the stop outside St Faith's School, having passed under the maze of wiring at the junction with Park Lane. *John Hughes collection*

Right: Bushbury Road, 1961. Sunbeam/Roe 452 is about to turn into Victoria Road on its way to town. On the corner can be seen a blue emergency police telephone box. Route 9 crosses from left to right in this view and continues up Prestwood Road. *John Hughes collection*

Left: With blinds incorrectly set for route 12A to Merry Hill via Bradmore (Merry Hill was 13 and Finchfield 12A), Sunbeam W4 443, still with its original Park Royal body, stands at the Low Hill terminus in Cannock Road on 12 April 1947. The Pear Tree pub that gave the terminus its name can be seen behind. *John Hughes collection*

Route 25: Fighting Cocks–Bilston–Willenhall

Right: Fighting Cocks (Ward Road) in June 1964. Sunbeam W4 416 arrives at the turning-circle, having completed the long run from Willenhall. The short wiring extension from Dudley Road up Goldthorn Hill to this new terminus was opened on 8 May 1949 in order to alleviate pressure on the parking loops at Dudding Road, where services 8, 25, 58 and 61 all either paused or terminated. *Author*

Left: The view along Church Street, Bilston, in the direction of Fighting Cocks, the photograph almost certainly taken from the tower of St Leonard's Church. *John Hughes collection*

Right: Guy BT 491 lays over at Bilston while on a Fighting Cocks working. Bilston depot is visible through the trees, while on the left of the picture can be seen the ex-Wolverhampton District Electric Tramways building. Still extant, the latter is now in use as a mosque! *John Hughes collection*

Right: With trafficator flashing, Guy BT 484 prepares to move away from the unloading point in Lichfield Street, Bilston, prior to making a right-hand turn into Mount Pleasant and drawing up at the layover point. Note the diamond crossing in the wiring loop, which allowed through trolleys on routes 2, 7 and 47 to pass unimpeded, without the need for points. *Author*

Left: Mount Pleasant, Bilston, in 1964, with Sunbeam W4 utility 417 departing for Willenhall. Standing outside the Globe Hotel, having arrived from Willenhall, another utility trolley pauses before continuing its inter-urban journey through Ettingshall and on to Fighting Cocks, where it will cross route 58 to Dudley before coming to rest at the Ward Road turning-circle. The green-painted waiting shelter showing route 24 for Willenhall is a throwback to the days of tram conversion and must have been there for many years, the correct route number, of course, being 25. *Author*

Left: Sunbeam F4 478 at the Willenhall layover point, by the Railway Tavern. Passing the Royal George public house, a Walsall Corporation trolleybus on route 29 negotiates the traffic island on the run to Wolverhampton. *Deryk Vernon collection*

Route 32: Wolverhampton–Oxbarn Avenue

Left: Guy BT 492, complete with grille badge, stands in the quiet backwater that is the town terminus in Chubb Street. *John Hughes collection*

Right: Victoria Square on 23 April 1960, with a motorised tricycle making a bold move between the trolleys. As Guy BT 603 clears the points 644, heading out of town, moves into the square from Railway Street and prepares to swing hard right across the road towards Lichfield Street. *John Hughes collection*

Left: Mid-afternoon, Sunbeam F4 622 has been parked up in Victoria Square on the Tettenhall through wires alongside a selection of ancient taxis whilst awaiting another turn of duty. The driver appears to have wound '22' on to the number blind in error. *John Hughes collection*

Left: Penn Road on 15 June 1956. Sunbeam F4 623 is about to turn right and start the long run down Coalway Road to the terminus. The hand-operated points at this location were biased for route 32, thus avoiding the need for any heroics from the conductor, who would otherwise have had to operate the pull cord (visible above the traffic light) and then dash across the busy junction to regain the comparative safety of the rear platform on 623. *John Hughes collection*

Right: A classic postwar view, recorded in November 1958. Guy BT 639 stands quietly at the Oxbarn Avenue terminus of route 32 (actually in Coalway Road, Oxbarn Avenue being to the right of the traffic island) as a wedding car pulls out behind and prepares to turn right at St Michael's Catholic Church. Altogether a peaceful scene, evoking memories of yesteryear and a time when life seemed less stressful than it is today. *Author's collection*

Left: The island at Oxbarn Avenue terminus was notoriously tight for trolleybuses to negotiate. Having unloaded outside the Catholic church (since replaced by a new, miniature version of Liverpool Cathedral), the trolleys would circumnavigate the traffic island and return to lay over just behind the photographer. Time appears to have stood still, and it is difficult to believe that this photograph was taken in 1962, more than a year after closure of the service. *John Hughes collection*

Depots

Left: Sunbeam F4 478 undergoing maintenance work in Cleveland Road depot. *Author's collection*

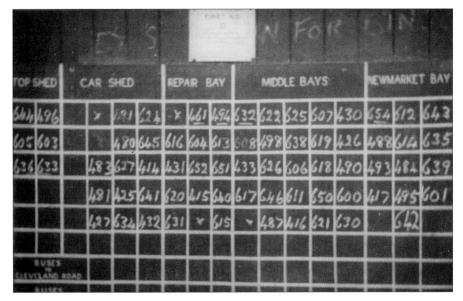

Left: The running board in Cleveland Road depot, showing daily bay allocations. Many familiar friends are there, including 415, withdrawn 8 August 1965 after the final summer on the Dudley route, 652, which worked the last Oxbarn Avenue service, plus 616 and 654, preserved in very different circumstances. Also present are 425, 426 and 427, which worked the final day's service. *Author's collection*

Right: Guy BT 484 on learner duty outside Cleveland Road depot. An instructor can be seen in the cab, giving the driver guidance as he negotiates his way past an eight-wheel flatbed lorry, all the time trying to remember where his booms are in relation to the pointwork and dead sections above him. *John Hughes collection*

Right: Cleveland Road depot in 1965, with several trolleys 'on shed' and 421 standing in the bay entrance. *Author*

Left: Cleveland Road in 1965. Standing against the kerb, Sunbeam W4 utility 406 awaits its next turn of duty, its booms angled wide to the overhead wires. It was common practice to treat this relatively quiet stretch of road as an extension of the depot, trolleys sometimes being parked almost in the middle of the roadway. *Author*

Left: An unidentified Sunbeam/Roe trolley is caught on camera in 1964 as it leaves Bilston depot and enters service heading towards Fraser Street; once there, it will make use of the reverser before returning to Mount Pleasant to work a scheduled service to Willenhall. *Author*

Wiring and electrical equipment

Left: A photograph taken at Chubb Street, off Victoria Square, showing the town terminus for routes 4 and 32 and a perfect display of professional wiring. The ex-LMS High Level railway station can be seen in the background. *John Hughes collection*

Below: A double-section feeder, mounted on a bracket arm, photographed *c*1945 opposite the Rose & Crown public house in Penn Road. *John Hughes collection*

Above: Its platform neatly positioned between the running-wires and the bracket arm of the traction pole, tower wagon No 8, a Guy Vixen purchased in 1947, stands outside the Chubb lock works whilst undertaking maintenance work. *John Hughes collection*

Above: **The beating heart of the Wolverhampton trolleybus system. This is the Corporation-owned main DC traction board, located on the ground floor of the power station in Commercial Road.** *John Hughes collection*

Right: **A pavement-mounted section pillar, believed to be in Newhampton Road. The men are mega-testing the side feeds for earth leakage.** *John Hughes collection*

5. The Beginning of the End

The decline of Wolverhampton's trolley-bus system began on 21 January 1961, which date saw the first route abandonment, of the 32 to/from Oxbarn Avenue via Coalway Road. At 11pm on that Saturday evening Guy BT 652 pulled out of Chubb Street for the last time for a final journey through the suburbs; no service was operated on the Sunday in view of the decision to close, coupled with the fact that the route was shadowed by motor-bus service 46, which could cover the light requirements on that day. A part-replacement motor-bus service was scheduled in the timetable, but the Corporation rarely if ever provided it.

No trolleybuses were withdrawn as a result of the abandonment, but on 28 February two succumbed to accident damage. Sunbeam 459 was taken to Cleveland Road depot, had its damaged parts removed and was prepared for rebuilding, but following a Council decision the vehicle was scrapped. Guy 647 had sustained rear-end damage, having backed into a rectifier substation while reversing out of Bilston depot. Neither would be disposed of until 18 September.

There was doubtful honour in the fact that route 32 had been the last to be introduced, back in February 1934. Its withdrawal gave Wulfrunians their first real indication that the trolleybus system that had served them faithfully for nearly half a century was to be axed by what seemed to be an indifferent Council decision that flew in the face of both public opinion and the proven facts of an economic, environmentally friendly mode of transport.

The inevitable sequel came on 10 March 1961, when it was announced in the *Express & Star* newspaper that the trolleybus system was to be systematically withdrawn and scrapped over the next few years. This followed a committee meeting held on 7 March, when the General Manager presented a major report on the future of the trolleybus system. His 22-page review was heavily biased against the retention of trolleybuses in any shape or form, advising that many of the problems foreseen in the 1957 report had now materialised, and appeared to cite the slightest of problems in the manufacturer's supply chain as an excuse to legitimise abandonment. Many of the statements were inaccurate, to say the least, and the impression was that a smokescreen was being put up to fool the ratepayers of Wolverhampton into believing they were seeing fair play in a decision that had, in reality, been all but

made, behind the scenes in Council. It must be remembered that this was the 1960s, when the population as a whole had more blind trust in authority, and it is unlikely that such a blatant subterfuge would succeed or be accepted today. An example of the negative tone was the mention of duplication of trolleybus routes by new motor-bus services such as that to Warstones Estate, the report stating that the layout of the new housing estate was not suitable for trolleybus operation; no explanation was given as to why the trolleybus service 32 was not extended in the first place. This new estate had wide, sweeping curved roads, and Councillors had either conveniently forgotten (or never visited) the back streets of route 9 around Great Brickkiln Street or Rayleigh Road, where narrow back streets of terraced houses and tight 90° turns into the next street, often on a hill, were the norm, yet trolleybus services operated with no problems at all.

In a television interview on *BBC Midlands News* a spokesman stated that, because the trolleybuses needed replacing and were not flexible enough for Wolverhampton's traffic conditions, it would make good economic sense to replace them with diesel buses. This comment ignored the hard facts that a sizable proportion of the fleet had only just received more modern bodywork and was in excellent mechanical and electrical condition. The inevitable protest letters were written to the newspaper, but these were largely ignored by the Council officers. The Transport Committee recommended that no more trolleybuses should be purchased and that, as they became due for major overhaul or renewal, the existing trolleys should be replaced by new motor buses, the recommendation being approved by the full Council at a meeting on 27 March; in these unseemly proceedings there was more than a hint of the ghost of Sir Charles Mander. In the event the system was to be scrapped with somewhat unnecessary and undue haste, the Council remaining tight-lipped over the whole business. Such was its haste to be rid of the trolleybuses that a number of safeguards written into the decision were blithely ignored. It was agreed that the trolleybuses be operated to the full extent of their useful life; scrapping a vehicle less than three years after a rebody does not meet this criterion. Walsall Corporation, alarmed at the decision, had been promised a minimum life of five years on the joint service. It was to be disappointed.

On Monday 23 January construction had commenced of a subway at the junction of Salop Street and School Street, effectively closing the junction of Victoria Street and Salop Street to all traffic, and for some weeks 21 Daimler CVG6 motor buses were hired in from Birmingham Corporation, at a charge of 6d per worked mile, to cover the suspension of services 4, 9, 11 and 32 until the resumption of trolleybus working on services 4, 9 and 11 on 22 May 1961. During this period a section of Penn Road, from Penn House Avenue to Pinfold Lane, was converted to dual carriageway, and the wiring replaced as new traction poles went in, the poles being repainted along the full length of Penn Road, though the Lea Road section was not so treated. This was the last big job to be undertaken on trolleybus overhead. Although it was advised as a suspension of service, trolleybuses were never restored to route 32, motor-bus service 46 to Warstones Estate being given an increased frequency to compensate.

The Penn Road junction points were removed quite quickly after the cessation of route 32, the Coalway Road wires being simply tied off to the nearest pole, without insulators, thus rendering virtually impossible any attempt at reactivating the section for tours. The rest of the section down to Oxbarn Avenue remained intact for more than 12 months, a long line of green traction poles standing as lonely sentinels, silently guarding the way and tracing out the route to the terminus, giving the eerie impression that a trolleybus might still appear at any moment. Perhaps the route refused to die … or was the Council having second thoughts and hedging its bets? Either way, one isolated traction pole, still in faded Corporation green, managed to survive in Coalway Road on the corner of Woodfield Avenue for many years after complete closure of the system.

In the light of the impending closures local resident John Hughes arranged a privately organised tour of the system, which ran on 7 August. Guy BT trolleybus 488 was chosen, being most appropriate, as it had just (on 31 July) received a full repaint. The tour included the Stubbs Road section, skilful manœuvring by the crew of Driver Harry Palmer and Conductor Wally Cox (plus the use of two retrieval poles) ensuring that no problems were encountered when crossing into Penn Road. Inspector Howard Davies was also present during the tour, which was the forerunner of many to come as the system contracted. However, this was to be the last occasion

SERVICE 32	WOLVERHAMPTON—OXBARN AVENUE (via Penn Road and Coalway Road)	TROLLEY BUS SERVICE

MONDAY TO FRIDAY

			AM	AM		AM	AM		PM	PM		
WOLVERHAMPTON	Chubb Street	dep.	6 30	7 0	every 8 minutes	8 44	8 58	every 20 minutes	1238	1 0	every 12 minutes	....
WOLVERHAMPTON	Oxbarn Avenue	arr.	6 44	7 14		8 58	9 12		1252	1 14		....

			AM	AM		AM	AM	AM		PM	PM			
WOLVERHAMPTON	Oxbarn Avenue	dep.	6 45	7 16	every 8 minutes	8 52	9 5	9 22	every 20 minutes	1 2	1 18	....	....	....
WOLVERHAMPTON	Chubb Street	arr.	6 59	7 30		9 6	9 19	9 36		1 16	1 32	....	....	....

			PM			PM	PM			PM				
WOLVERHAMPTON	Chubb Street	dep.	4 0	every 8 minutes		6 16	6 30	every 30 minutes		11 0	....	....	....	....
WOLVERHAMPTON	Oxbarn Avenue	arr.	4 14			6 30	6 44			1114	....	....	....	....

				PM	PM		PM	PM		PM		
WOLVERHAMPTON	Oxbarn Avenue	dep.	every 12 minutes	4 6	4 16	every 8 minutes	6 32	6 45	every 30 minutes	1115	....	....
WOLVERHAMPTON	Chubb Street	arr.		4 20	4 30		6 46	6 59		1129	....	....

SATURDAY

			AM	AM	AM		PM	PM		PM	PM		
WOLVERHAMPTON	Chubb Street	dep.	6 30	6 45	7 0	every 12 minutes	6 0	6 18	every 20 minutes	1038	11 0	....	....
WOLVERHAMPTON	Oxbarn Avenue	arr.	6 44	6 59	7 14		6 14	6 32		1052	1114	....	....

			AM	AM	AM		PM	PM		PM	PM		
WOLVERHAMPTON	Oxbarn Avenue	dep.	6 45	7 0	7 18	every 12 minutes	6 6	6 22	every 20 minutes	11 2	1116	....	....
WOLVERHAMPTON	Chubb Street	arr.	6 59	7 14	7 32		6 20	6 36		1116	1130	....	....

SUNDAY

			PM		PM									
WOLVERHAMPTON	Chubb Street	dep.	2 0	every 30 minutes	11 0	....	....	....	....	....	....	....	....	....
WOLVERHAMPTON	Oxbarn Avenue	arr.	2 14		1114	....	....	....	....	....	....	....	....	....

			PM		PM									
WOLVERHAMPTON	Oxbarn Avenue	dep.	2 15	every 30 minutes	1115	....	....	....	....	....	....	....	....	....
WOLVERHAMPTON	Chubb Street	arr.	2 29		1129	....	....	....	....	....	....	....	....	....

Above: Guy Vixen tower wagon No 7 seen on the Penn Road near Pennhouse Avenue in 1961, during realignment work on the overhead as a result of road-widening on this stretch and the creation of a dual carriageway. *John Hughes collection*

WOLVERHAMPTON CORPORATION
TRANSPORT DEPARTMENT

WARSTONES ESTATE −
− UNDERHILL ESTATE

SERVICE No. 46.

Commencing Wednesday, 24th May, 1961,

the Trolley Bus Service to Oxbarn Avenue (Service 32) will be withdrawn and the following revised service between Warstones Estate and Underhill Estate will be introduced. The picking up point for the Oxbarn Avenue Service in Queen Square will be discontinued, the nearest alternative being Lichfield Street (opposite the Art Gallery). The Town terminal point en route from Warstones Estate to Underhill Estate will be Chubb Street, not Railway Street.

MONDAY TO FRIDAY

			AM	AM	AM	OX	AM		AM		AM	AM	AM	AM	AM	AM	
WARSTONES ESTATE	Enville Road	dep.	....	6 25	....	6 45	....	6 58	every	8 42	8 50	8 59	9 6	9 14	9 23	every
WOLVERHAMPTON	Chubb Street	„	6 40	6 45	6 53	7 1	7 9	7 17	8	9 1	9 12	9 17	9 27	9 33	9 42	15
UNDERHILL ESTATE	Underhill Lane	arr.	6 56	7 1	7 9	7 17	7 25	7 33	minutes	9 17	9 28	....	9 43	....	9 58	minutes

			AM	AM	AM	AM	AM	AM		AM	AM	AM	AM	AM	AM	
UNDERHILL ESTATE	Underhill Lane	dep.	....	.... OX	....	....	....	6 42	every	8 34	8 42	8 46	8 57	9 5	9 16	every
WOLVERHAMPTON	Railway Street	„	6 5	6 30	6 35	6 42	6 50	6 58	8	8 50	9 2	9 2	9 17	9 21	9 32	15
WARSTONES ESTATE	Enville Road	arr.	6 23	6 44	6 53	7 0	7 8	7 16	minutes	9 8	9 20	....	9 35	....	9 50	minutes

			PM	PM	PM	PM	PM		PM	PM	PM	PM		PM	PM	PM
WARSTONES ESTATE	Enville Road	dep.	1253	....	1 8	1 23	1 35	every	3 25	....	3 36	3 46	every	6 42	6 50	6 58
WOLVERHAMPTON	Chubb Street	„	1 12	1 21	1 32	1 43	1 54	11	3 44	3 49	3 57	4 5	8	7 1	7 10	7 17
UNDERHILL ESTATE	Underhill Lane	arr.	1 28	1 37	1 48	1 59	2 10	minutes	4 0	4 5	4 13	4 21	minutes	7 17	7 26	....

			PM	PM	PM	PM	PM		PM	PM	PM	PM	PM		PM	PM
UNDERHILL ESTATE	Underhill Lane	dep.	1246	....	1 1	1 16	1 30	every	3 9	....	3 20	3 30	3 36	3 46	every	6 34
WOLVERHAMPTON	Railway Street	„	1 2	1 13	1 24	1 35	1 46	11	3 25	3 30	3 38	3 46	3 54	4 2	8	6 50
WARSTONES ESTATE	Enville Road	arr.	1 20	1 31	1 42	1 53	2 4	minutes	3 43	3 48	3 56	4 4	4 12	4 20	minutes	7 8

			PM	PM	PM	PM		PM	PM	PM	PM				
WARSTONES ESTATE	Enville Road	dep.	7 6	7 14	7 21	7 36	every	1036	1051	11 4	1119	....	....	....
WOLVERHAMPTON	Chubb Street	„	7 25	7 40	7 40	7 55	15	1055	1110	1123	1138	....	....	....
UNDERHILL ESTATE	Underhill Lane	arr.	7 41	7 56	....	8 11	minutes	1111	....	....	....	....	....	....

			PM	PM	PM	PM	PM	PM	PM		PM	PM	PM			
UNDERHILL ESTATE	Underhill Lane	dep.	6 42	6 50	6 58	7 6	7 14	7 22	7 29	every	1044	1059	1112	....	....	....
WOLVERHAMPTON	Railway Street	„	7 0	7 6	7 15	7 22	7 30	7 38	7 45	15	11 0	1115	1128	....	....	....
WARSTONES ESTATE	Enville Road	arr.	7 18	....	7 33	....	7 48	....	8 3	minutes	1118	....	....	....	....	....

SATURDAY

			AM	OX	AM	AM		AM	AM	AM	AM	AM		PM	PM	PM
WARSTONES ESTATE	Enville Road	dep.	6 25	6 45	....	7 0	every	8 39	8 48	....	9 1	9 14	every	5 47	5 56	6 5
WOLVERHAMPTON	Chubb Street	„	6 44	6 59	7 8	7 19	11	8 58	9 7	9 15	9 24	9 33	9	6 6	6 15	6 25
UNDERHILL ESTATE	Underhill Lane	arr.	7 0	7 15	7 24	7 35	minutes	9 14	9 23	9 31	9 40	9 49	minutes	6 22	6 31	6 41

			AM	AM	AM	AM	AM	AM		AM	AM	AM	AM	AM	AM	
UNDERHILL ESTATE	Underhill Lane	dep.	....	.... OX	....	....	....	6 42	every	8 34	....	8 45	8 56	9 7	9 19	....
WOLVERHAMPTON	Railway Street	„	6 5	6 30	6 38	6 45	7 0	7 11	7 22	11	8 50	8 59	9 8	9 17	9 26	9 35
WARSTONES ESTATE	Enville Road	arr.	6 23	6 44	6 56	7 3	7 18	7 29	7 40	minutes	9 8	9 17	9 26	9 35	9 44	9 53

SATURDAY continued / **SUNDAY**

			PM	PM	PM	PM		PM	PM	PM	PM			AM	AM	PM
WARSTONES ESTATE	Enville Road	dep.	6 13	6 21	6 28	6 36	every	1036	1051	11 4	1119	....	....	9 0	9 45	1040
WOLVERHAMPTON	Chubb Street	„	6 40	6 40	6 47	6 55	15	1055	1110	1123	1138	....	....	9 19	10 4	1058
UNDERHILL ESTATE	Underhill Lane	arr.	6 56	....	....	7 11	minutes	1111	....	....	....	....	....			

				PM	PM	PM	PM	PM	PM		PM	PM	PM	AM	AM	PM
UNDERHILL ESTATE	Underhill Lane	dep.	every	6 1	6 10	6 19	6 28	6 37	6 44	every	1044	1059	1112	....	....	....
WOLVERHAMPTON	Railway Street	„	9	6 17	6 30	6 35	6 45	6 53	7 0	15	11 0	1115	1128	8 40	9 20	1020
WARSTONES ESTATE	Enville Road	arr.	minutes	6 35	6 48	....	7 2	....	7 18	minutes	1118	....	....	8 58	9 38	1038

SUNDAY continued

			AM	AM	PM	PM	PM	PM		PM	PM	PM	PM			
WARSTONES ESTATE	Enville Road	dep.	1140	1220	1 0	1 36	2 6	every	1036	1051	11 4	1119	....	....	....
WOLVERHAMPTON	Chubb Street	„	1120	1159	1239	1 19	1 55	2 25	15	1055	1110	1123	1138	....	....
UNDERHILL ESTATE	Underhill Lane	arr.	1136	1215	1255	1 35	2 11	2 41	minutes	1111	....	....	....	....	....

			AM	AM	PM	PM	PM	PM	PM	PM		PM	PM	p.m.	
UNDERHILL ESTATE	Underhill Lane	dep.	....	1140	1220	1259	....	1 40	....	2 14	every	2 44	1044	1059	1112
WOLVERHAMPTON	Railway Street	„	1115	1156	1236	1 15	1 45	2 0	2 15	2 30	2 45	3 0	15	11 0	1115	1128
WARSTONES ESTATE	Enville Road	arr.	1133	1214	1254	1 33	2 3	2 18	2 33	2 48	3 3	3 18	minutes	1118	....	....

OX : To or from Oxbarn Avenue only

FARE LIST: The Fare Stage known as "Railway Street' will read "Chubb Street or Railway Street".

R. H. ADDLESEE, M.Inst. T., M.Inst.T.A.,
General Manager.

Wolverhampton Corporation Transport Department,
Cleveland Road, Wolverhampton.
May, 1961.

Printed by PEDLEY & BLACKHAM. (Printers) LTD., 34/35 DUDLEY ROAD. W'TON.

on which Stubbs Road wiring was energised, this being isolated again just a few days later.

In September an order was placed with Guy Motors for 150 motor buses as replacements for the trolleybuses, with delivery phased over several years. All were to be Guy Arabs with the exception of two new Wulfrunian models that were to be taken on a trial basis.

During the course of 1961 the overhead pointwork in the town centre, and in many other locations further out of town, was fitted with electric 'frogs' (points in railway language) working off contact skates inserted in the overhead wires, immediately in front of the points. This facility was considered necessary to ease operation in and around the town centre, especially at busy road junctions, where the ever-increasing volume of traffic made life difficult for trolleybus drivers — not to mention conductors, who appeared to lead charmed lives as they weaved around vehicles on foot to operate pull cords on traction poles before returning to their trolleys.

Current, when drawn, as the trolley head passed under the skate, would energise a solenoid, activating the point blade movement. Indicator boxes displaying twin clear bulbs were placed on adjoining traction poles to give the driver visual confirmation that his booms had taken the correct route divergence. Unless local road conditions dictated otherwise, points would usually be set for the straight exit, and drivers would coast through with no power on the pedal. To change this for a left- or right-hand divergence it was necessary for the driver to slow to 5mph and then, with the handbrake held loosely back, power through the point on one or two notches of his pedal. As he cleared the junction the indicator light would go out to indicate that the trolley head had made contact with the 'striker' and that the blades had returned to the straight position.

The occasional failure was not unknown, with points staying open and the indicator light still on. Following drivers would then have to stop their trolleys and walk over to a traction pole, where an emergency cord could be pulled to reset the point blades, though a following trolley taking the same route could coast through the junction, and this would usually activate the reset mechanism. Both indicator lights showing invariably meant that the mechanism had failed, one boom taking each route — an emergency stop being needed by the quick-thinking driver to avoid the inevitable chaos that could ensue, with booms detaching from the wires and swinging outboard of the vehicle. Elsewhere on the system manually operated points remained, these being operated on a pull-and-hold basis and returning to the original setting upon release of the cord.

Left: The corner of Coalway Road and Riley Crescent one afternoon in May 1961 as two young girls make their way home from nearby Woodfield Avenue School. It looks as though a trolleybus might appear at any moment, yet the photograph was taken four months after the closure on 21 January. *John Hughes collection*

Below: The 488 tour, organised by John Hughes. With Driver Harry Palmer at the wheel, newly repainted Guy BT 488 heads along Stubbs Road towards Penn Road on 7 August 1961. In the background can be seen the Lea Road terminus. *Author's collection*

Wednesday 14 February 1962 saw the entry into service of the final rebodied Sunbeam W4, No 445 (although this was to have a short life in its new form, being withdrawn following an accident on 18 January 1965). Sunbeam F4 609 was withdrawn on 28 February, being one of four F4s and two Guy BTs due for overhaul and considered surplus to requirements. Sister vehicle 623 had been withdrawn the previous month following an accident on the Penn Road. It was the first of its class to suffer this fate and would not run again.

Data available for the year ending 31 March 1962 gives the following information:

Total trolleybus miles run: 5,246,523
Average number of trolleybuses
in daily use: 119
Miles of route traversable: 47.07
Average daily miles run per vehicle: 121

Between February 1962 and May 1963 a further eight second-hand trolleybuses, this time of the Sunbeam F4 type with 56-seat Park Royal bodywork, were acquired by Walsall Corporation. Purchased from Ipswich, they were numbered 344-7/51-4 and entered service on route 29, displacing the ex-Hastings vehicles to local workings in much the same way that the latter had replaced the earlier F4 trolleys.

Early in 1962 it was announced that a Royal visit was to be made on 24 May by HM Queen Elizabeth II. Great efforts were made by the Borough Council to ensure that the town was suitably adorned for the visit, with local schoolchildren to be present along the proposed route from the ex-GWR Low Level station to the Royal School on Compton Road, and the Parks Department arranging for the concrete traffic islands *en route*, to be 'planted' with

newly laid turf and flowers. The Transport Department would also play its part, with detailed schedules covering the movement of all buses prior to and for the duration of the visit. Termination points were agreed for trolleybus services conflicting with the route that the Royal party would take, and from 10am inspectors were deployed in force to supervise the arrangements. In some locations extended jump leads, supported on spare retriever poles, were used to allow deviation from the overhead alignment and assist in turning trolleybuses around. The operation was broken down as follows:

From the south
Services 4, 9, 11
Trolleys were stopped at the bottom of Victoria Street and made a three-point turn, reversing into St Johns Street with the aid of gravity, assisted by hand propulsion from the inspectors.

Services 2, 7, 47
Vehicles arriving from Bilston and Darlaston were held in Victoria Square, outside the Victoria Hotel, some being turned back to operate a limited shuttle service to Darlaston.

From the west
Services 12, 13
Those trolleys entering town from Bradmore used the newly constructed lay-by alongside the eye infirmary at Chapel Ash and were also turned by hand. The lay-by had been installed as part of the recently revised road layout at Chapel Ash. Previously all traffic negotiated a small island, where the wires for Tettenhall and Bradmore diverged; after the reconstruction, which necessitated the removal of the traffic island and the introduction of traffic lights and multiple lanes, an electric point, with indicator box, was installed alongside the outbound bus stop at the foot of

Left: Roe-bodied Sunbeam W4 424 forms a queue with two Walsall Corporation trolleybuses (including 347, an ex-Ipswich Sunbeam F4 with a Park Royal body) waiting to leave for Wolverhampton. The Ipswich trolleys replaced the Hastings vehicles on joint route 29, the displaced trolleys being transferred to local services. *John Hughes collection*

Left: The date is Thursday 24 May 1962, the occasion the visit to Wolverhampton of HM Queen Elizabeth II. For the duration of the visit all traffic was stopped from entering the town centre, trolleybuses being turned short (in some cases by hand) at strategic points around the town. As a white-gloved policeman holds back the traffic, inspectors and mechanics assist in turning Sunbeam F4 624 in St John's Street at the foot of Victoria Street to enable the trolley to return to Penn. Extended jump leads were also used to assist in moving trolleys into adjacent side streets. No 624 would be withdrawn just over a year later, with the closure to trolleybuses of the Penn and Penn Fields routes on 9 June 1963. *Author's collection*

Darlington Street, with twin sets of wires running through Chapel Ash to the divergence point of the two routes.

Service 1
This was stopped short of Chapel Ash in Tettenhall Road, at its junction with Connaught Road, trolleys again being turned by hand.

Services 2, 7
Inbound workings from Whitmore Reans were stopped and queued in Waterloo Road, there being no convenient turning point.

From the north
Service 3
Trolleybuses arriving from Fordhouses were able to reach their town-centre loading-point in Wulfruna Street, being then lined up outside the wholesale market.

From the east
Services 3, 9, 12, 13
Incoming trolleys from Bushbury and Low Hill were stopped in a long queue near the top of Stafford Street, Amos Lane trolleys managing to get a few yards further, into Whitmore Street, where they parked in their regular spot. With Wulfruna Street getting congested, the decision was taken to divert any remaining trolleybuses returning from Fordhouses into Stafford Street, by way of the emergency wiring in Lower Stafford Street, originally intended as a diversion when football spectators were leaving the Molineux ground in Waterloo Road.

Services 6, 59
Wednesfield services stopped short of the overbridge at the low-level railway station, where the trolleys remained until services resumed.

Services to/from Walsall and Dudley were largely unaffected, due to their more remote loading points.

One amusing incident resulting from the visit involved the driver of Roe-bodied Sunbeam 448, inbound on service 12 from Finchfield. On arrival in Lichfield Street he found Princes Square and the top of Stafford Street to be already closed to traffic, so by a quick change of wires he continued down to Victoria Square and manœuvred his trolley into the centre of the square, where he parked up in the lay-by loop wiring normally used by Tettenhall trolleys. As a result of this move, when services re-started in the afternoon he was able to leave town more quickly than the trolleys held in Stafford Street and make his way back to Finchfield without delay.

In July 1962 the emergency connection wires in Stubbs Road were lifted. In part this was brought about by the fact that

Left: On the occasion of the visit of HM Queen Elizabeth II on 24 May 1962 arrangements were made for the stopping and turning-short of trolleybuses due to road closures in the town centre. Here we see a row of inbound trolleys, from Bushbury, Low Hill and Amos Lane, held at the top of Stafford Street (approximately where the ring road now crosses), just short of Whitmore Street. *Author's collection*

Left: As the day progressed, incoming trolleybuses from Fordhouses were diverted up Lower Stafford Street to avoid excessive congestion in Wulfruna Street. *Author's collection*

routes 4 and 11 were facing probable abandonment in the near future, but it also allowed for the removal of wiring in Worcester Street, necessary to permit construction of a new ring road.

The end of the year was to see special peak-hour relief workings thinned out. Among the journeys withdrawn were two daily trips from Wolverhampton to Dudley via Bilston and Fighting Cocks, at 8am and 5pm, and a further working from Bilston to Willenhall via Wolverhampton, at 8am.

With abandonment looming, maintenance was now being kept to a minimum, and in the town centre the overhead in general began to take on a somewhat bedraggled appearance, with slack wiring adding to the difficulties of driving through the streets. However, the announcement of a withdrawal from the market by one of the two remaining suppliers of overhead fittings galvanised the

Transport Department into renewing overhead fittings on the Willenhall route, any serviceable parts recovered being held as spares for the rest of the system. With the closure of Alfred Wiseman, of Birmingham, British Insulated Calender Cables (BICC) was now the only company still manufacturing overhead wire. The decision was taken that the remaining 8ft-wide trolleybuses should receive 'minimum' maintenance and that any such trolley sustaining major accident damage or suffering serious mechanical failure was to be withdrawn from service.

In due course there appeared in local newspapers the anticipated announcement to the effect that, on Sunday 9 June 1963, trolleybus services 4 to Penn Fields and 11 to Penn would be withdrawn. The final departures from town, at 11pm, were attended by members of a fledgling enthusiast group that was eventually to form

part of the National Trolleybus Association (NTA), this being a gesture that would become a feature of closures on the Wolverhampton system and, indeed, nationwide. As trolleybus 498 prepared to leave Chubb Street a member of the public fixed to the front of the vehicle a placard bearing the inscription 'THE LAST PENN FIELDS TROLLEYBUS'; this was removed by an inspector just prior to departure at 11pm. Out at Penn terminus Driver R. Mason arrived a little after 11.15pm with 606, working the final journey under wires along the Penn Road. Following these closures 15 trolleybuses were withdrawn and delicensed. The wiring was dismantled over a period of time.

In the latter half of June came an announcement in the local newspaper that there were insufficient motor buses available to replace the next trolleybus route due for abandonment, this being cross-

Above: Railway Street, Wolverhampton on the last day of operation. Guy BT 639 rests quietly in Railway Street, outside the Chubb lock works building on Sunday 9 June 1963. The wiring that enabled transfers from Park Lane depot to Cleveland Road can be seen on this side of the road; it was not used in daily service by any routes. *Author*

town service 9 (Jeffcock Road–Amos Lane). It was decided instead to substitute route 1 to Tettenhall, the axe falling on 30 June, with Sunbeam F4 No 622 performing the last rites on this most prestigious of routes. As predicted, there was no effort made by the Council to mark the event in any way, despite the fact that in times past it had chosen to bask in its pride of Tettenhall as the 'élite' route so beloved of certain Council members, not to mention the fact that this had also been the first tram route to be operated by the Corporation.

August 1963 saw the removal of the Church Road loop at Oxley and an extensive stretch of Stafford Road upgraded to dual carriageway, slewing of the overhead wiring allowing services to continue whilst the road was laid.

Route 9 had remained firmly in the next position on the closure list. By now the second stage of the inner ring road was well underway, and construction works had steadily encroached to the edge of Great Brickkiln Street, requiring the removal of overhead wiring. However, there was to be a brief reprieve in the unlikely form of a shortage of replacement motor buses. As a result only partial closure was effected on Sunday 29 September, when the section from town to Jeffcock Road was severed; the remaining section, between town and Amos Lane, was renumbered 88 and now

operated from the top of Stafford Street, using existing wiring to turn at Stafford Street island, the outbound loading stop being used as the starting point. Whitmore Street wiring fell into disuse but was retained for depot movements. No 423 was the last trolley to work the through journey to Jeffcock Road, 475 covering the last through run to Amos Lane.

Four trolleybuses were withdrawn as a result of the closure. All wiring was now cleared from the western side of town, to allow construction of the new ring road to commence, and the road works meant that, for its first few weeks of operation, the replacement motor-bus service (which retained route number 9) had on its outbound journey to divert via Worcester Street and part of the new ring road before regaining the route at Great Brickkiln Street

The reprieve for Amos Lane was to be short, for just five weeks later, on 3 November, service 88 was withdrawn, together with all operations on routes 6, 12, 13 and 59, resulting in the loss of all trolleybus services to Merryhill, Finchfield, Low Hill and Wednesfield. No 451 made the final trip from Stafford Street to Amos Lane,

444 covering the last working of the difficult Finchfield reverser, 616 working out to Merry Hill and 446 performing the last rites on the Wednesfield service. This was a savage blow to those fighting to retain the remaining trolleybus services and was to see the greatest number of routes withdrawn at any one time. No fewer than 25 trolleys were removed from service.

On 30 November trolleybus 616 was purchased jointly by an enthusiast organisation, the Wolverhampton Trolleybus Group, and the Midlands branch of the Railway Preservation Society, for preservation. A 1949 Sunbeam F4, with 8ft-wide Park Royal bodywork, it was unusual in having double reduction gearing on the rear axle and was instantly recognisable from the distinctive high-pitched whine emanating from the rear of the vehicle. Withdrawn on 3 November after service on route 59, it was placed for safe storage in Park Lane depot, where it was to remain for some time after sale.

Postwar years had seen an increased interest in trolleybuses, with tours of existing systems organised by various groups, one of the first being in Wolverhampton,

Above: Whitmore Street, Wolverhampton, with the crew of Sunbeam W4 423 waiting to depart with the last trolleybus to Jeffcock Road, on 29 September 1963. *John Hughes collection*

Above: Sunbeam F4 475 waiting at Jeffcock Road on 29 September 1963 with the last through run across town to Amos Lane. *John Hughes collection*

Above: Sunbeam F4 471 waits at the Stafford Street loading point on the short-lived (five-week) renumbered service to Amos Lane. *Author's collection*

Above: Merry Hill terminus on 3 November 1963. The last trolleybus, Sunbeam F4 616, has just arrived, and a photographic record is being made. Holding the banner are John Hughes and David Smith. *John Hughes collection*

by the Southern Counties Touring Society on 3 June 1951. On 11 June 1961 Walsall Corporation 870 was hired by the Tramway Museum Society and, with Wolverhampton Corporation's agreement, worked through to Fighting Cocks via Bilston using the wiring on route 25. The journey continued to Cleveland Road depot and was followed by a return to Walsall. On 24 March 1963 the Nottingham Trolleybus Group hired Roe-bodied 439 on a farewell tour of the system. Then, on 19 May, the Wolverhampton Trolleybus Group operated a tour using 616 and 433 (both of which would eventually be preserved, albeit in very different circumstances), which covered virtually all of the surviving routes. From time to time trolleybuses, usually in immaculate condition, were also hired for private functions and associated trips.

On 22 September 1963 a very different tour was operated, using Walsall 869, one of 22 30ft-long Sunbeam F4A trolleys with 70-seat Willowbrook bodywork, introduced between 1954 and 1956 in response to the 1954 Walsall Corporation Act, which legalised operation of 30ft two-axle trolleybuses in Britain. Starting from Walsall bus station and handled throughout by Walsall driver Gilbert Dunn, the tour worked over the recently opened Beechdale extension. The party then set off for Lower Farm via Bloxwich, following this with what was the longest possible through trolleybus journey in the West Midlands. From Lower Farm 869 travelled through Bloxwich to Walsall, and then on to Fighting Cocks via Willenhall and Bilston. At Fighting Cocks the spur was used to gain access to the Dudley wires, and the journey continued on through Sedgley to terminate in Stone Street, Dudley. Leaving Dudley, 869 travelled to Cleveland Road depot by way of the Green Dragon circle, then down to Merryhill — out via Railway Street and Broad Street, back via Lichfield Street (the Chubb Street loop being reluctantly omitted due to clearance problems) — before finally returning to Walsall. The first — and only — Walsall trolleybus to reach Worcestershire under wires, the vehicle was accompanied bt R. Edgley Cox, General Manager of Walsall Corporation Transport Department.

On Boxing Day 1963 trolley 419 was involved in an accident, thus becoming the first Roe-bodied vehicle to be withdrawn, while on 20 January 1964 601 also suffered accident damage, never to run again. The following day there was a thick fog, and 438/40/50 were all involved in collisions on the Fordhouses route. All three vehicles received damage to the front, 450 additionally to the rear. Whilst 438 and 440 underwent repairs, 450 was written off, although its bodywork was a mere two years old.

The upgrading of part of the Stafford Road to dual carriageway was now approaching completion, and with work ahead of schedule the abandonment date for route 3 to Fordhouses was brought forward from March to January, the cross-town working to Bushbury ceasing at the same time. Thus the additional costs of new overhead equipment that had been used to slew the wiring across the carriageway during the road-widening scheme would effectively be wasted. It had been hoped that there would be a breathing space, with closure delayed to recoup some of the cost involved, but to no avail.

The morning of Sunday 26 January 1964 had a chill in the air, as well as a damp mist that was to persist until the evening. There began a complicated set of manœuvres which were to last the day. All through the morning some 20 trolleybuses, both Park Royal 8ft and '402' utilities, were backed out of Cleveland Road depot and, after de-wiring, were coasted down to form a queue at the bottom of Hospital Street. From there they were towed across Bilston Street by overhead repair wagon and lined up on waste ground in Oxford Street. At the same time, to take their place, 20 of the modern Roe-bodied vehicles were worked up from Park Lane depot via the 'up' wiring in Railway Street, used only for transfer movements; trolley 450 also

Above: On 11 June 1961 the Tramway Museum Society operated a tour using Walsall Corporation 870, a 30ft-long Sunbeam F4A fitted with Willowbrook bodywork. With authority granted by Wolverhampton Corporation, it ran from Walsall to Fighting Cocks using Wolverhampton wiring via route 25 and using the west–south spur at the Parkfield Road / Dudley Road junction, returning to Walsall through Wolverhampton via Cleveland Road depot wiring. It is seen here at Willenhall, having just turned onto route 25.
No doubt the driver of native Sunbeam 485 was more than a little surprised at the arrival of 870! *John Hughes collection*

Below: Walsall Corporation 870 at Fighting Cocks loop on 11 June 1961, in the company of two Wolverhampton trolleybuses including Guy BT 607. The group of Walsall Corporation officials posed in front of 870 include that undertaking's radical and enthusiastic General Manager, R. Edgley Cox, in pullover and sports jacket. *John Hughes collection*

Above: Enthusiasts gather for a group photograph at Penn Fields terminus on 24 March 1963. The Wolverhampton Trolleybus Group operated a full tour of the system using 616, a Sunbeam F4 with Park Royal bodywork, and 433, a Sunbeam W4, originally with a Park Royal body but by now sporting a new Roe body. *John Hughes collection*

came up from Park Lane but was worked through to Oxford Street, to join its companions. This left only four trolleys at Park Lane, and these worked the Sunday service for the rest of that day. As evening approached the service was supplemented by a motor bus; this would have covered the last working, but after consultation between well-wishers and the duty inspector the schedules were switched to ensure that a trolleybus would make the last trip out to Fordhouses. Enthusiasts turned out in force, travelling out from Wulfruna Street to Fordhouses terminus, where 448 was duly photographed before returning to town for the last time.

Last vehicles coming in that evening from Fordhouses were unhooked from the wiring in Wulfruna Street, coasted across the deserted Princes Square into Broad Street and, after re-attachment to the overhead, driven direct to Cleveland Road depot via Railway Street. Meanwhile 453 and 439 had worked out along Cannock Road and through Park Village before turning up Park Lane with the last trolleybuses to Bushbury Hill. The following day 428 and three other trolleybuses were worked across town in a sad convoy to their new (albeit temporary) home at Cleveland Road, and (the aforementioned 616 excepted) Park Lane depot was devoid of trolleybuses.

By the start of 1964 the overhead had been removed from Penn and Penn Fields, and very little remained on the Tettenhall route. By March all wiring had been lifted

Above: A unique tour was run on 22 September 1963 when, with agreement from the transport departments of Walsall and Wolverhampton, Walsall Corporation 869 was worked through from Lower Farm Estate, outside Bloxwich, to Dudley, travelling via Walsall, Willenhall, Bilston, Fighting Cocks and Sedgley. This was the longest through journey possible in Britain by trolleybus and would be the one and only time that a Walsall trolley entered Worcestershire. No 869 is pictured at the end of its long journey, at the Stone Street terminus in Dudley, along with Wolverhampton service trolley 431. *John Hughes collection*

Above: Fordhouses terminus on 21 January 1964, with Sunbeam 448 about to work the last trip back to town before transferring the same night to Cleveland Road depot. *John Hughes collection*

from the Tettenhall route, Chapel Ash and the lower part of Darlington Street; also gone were two of the four sets of wiring through Queen Square and one of the two outward lines in the upper part of Darlington Street. The Jeffcock Road wiring had been removed from Victoria Street to the junction with the new ring road, and the Broad Street connection with the Wednesfield route had been severed.

One evening early in March the mass of wiring at the three-way junction in Cannock Road was tackled: using two tower wagons — a Guy Warrior and a Guy Vixen — the main junction was removed within one hour, several of the better items being saved for reuse. The end of the month saw the removal of more overhead from the now-depleted Fordhouses section and all of that in Lower Stafford Street.

Most of the trolleys dumped in Oxford Street were moved to Park Lane depot on the morning of 8 March. Had the overhead been left in place for just a little while longer, they could have been driven across town and out to Park Lane depot instead of being towed along Cannock Road under the wiring they had used two months earlier.

Above: With the closure of route 3 (Fordhouses–Bushbury Hill) Park Lane would cease to operate trolleybuses. On the morning of Sunday 26 January 1964 some 20 Roe-bodied trolleybuses worked up from Park Lane depot to Cleveland Road, via the inbound wiring in Railway Street, to replace ageing Sunbeam and Guy 8ft-wide vehicles. Throughout the day the redundant 8ft-wide trolleys were backed out of Cleveland Road depot, coasted around the corner into Hospital Street and then towed across Bilston Street to a patch of waste ground in Oxford Street. Guy BT 493 is seen passing the Fox & Goose public house as it approaches its destination. *Author*

Left: Another trolleybus arrives behind the towing wagon to join the growing band of vehicles. *Author*

Right: Unloved and unwanted (by the Corporation), a sizeable collection of once-gleaming trolleybuses huddle together on the Oxford Street pound. The back row includes Nos 627, 601 and 636. All have suffered damage to the rear windows. *Author*

Left: Two Sunbeam W4 utilities stand at the Oxford Street pound, awaiting their fate in company with an elderly single-deck motor bus. The leading trolley appears to have suffered severe damage to one of its booms, almost certainly sealing its fate at this time. *Author*

Above: A desolate scene at the back of Park Lane depot in 1964 as withdrawn trolleybuses stand forlornly together next to the boundary fence. With the closure of cross-town route 3 on Sunday 26 January Park Lane ceased to be an active trolleybus depot and, notwithstanding the motor-bus allocation, took on a neglected and uncared-for appearance. *Author*

Right: March 1964. Overhead crews are busy removing wiring from the junction of Cannock Road and Park Lane, following the abandonment of route 3 and the transfer of the remaining trolleybuses to Cleveland Road depot. *John Hughes collection*

6. The Last Stand

Wolverhampton's trolleybus system was now left to fight on with just the heavy-weight routes to Darlaston, Walsall and Dudley still connected by the umbilical cord of cross-country route 25. The trolleybus system had long since established itself in the consciousness of the town, and it had been hoped by many people that some form of sense would now prevail, as, with the town centre now virtually clear of services and with only the Whitmore Reans wiring passing through Queen Square, the remaining routes, which in 1964 were still heavily trafficked and were ideal for trolleybus operation, could be retained and further modernised. Sadly this was destined not to happen.

The wiring on the Dudley route had rapidly corroded over the years, and the Corporation's Overhead Line Superintendent, Mr Eric Ball, had to have the route re-wired. Guy 'Warrior' tower wagon No 2 was used for much of the work, carried out in the spring of 1964.

The annual NTA tour took place on 5 April. On this occasion Sunbeam W4/Park Royal 408 was used and, being one of the '402' class of rebodied utility vehicles, proved a popular choice. Starting from the Victoria Square central refuges, the tour included all available wiring on routes 2, 47, 25, 8, 58 and 61, including the Fighting Cocks west–south spur, along with a visit to the Fraser Street reverser prior to a run through to Darlaston. During the return leg the booms were lowered at the junction with Great Bridge Road, so that 408 could be manually pushed round the corner, and then reconnected to the overhead and worked around the terminus loop. On reaching Bilston depot 408 was posed alongside two other trolleys, Roe-bodied 432 and 461, an 8ft-wide Sunbeam F4, illustrating the three styles still in use.

On 26 April, at 8.30pm, there was a wiring breakdown outbound at the bottom of Horseley Fields, affecting routes 5 and 29, when a wooden spacing bar failed and in separating allowed the wires to drift apart. The repair crew were soon on site, but, this being a busy Saturday evening, queues of trolleybuses soon built up in each direction. Under the direction of an inspector trolley booms were swung across and placed on the up wires (with the bamboo retriever pole still attached), and vehicles worked 'wrong line' around the fault, conductors walking behind each trolley to steady the retriever. This manœuvre, made alternately with inbound services from Walsall, enabled a flow of trolleys to be maintained.

Opposite top: Sunbeam W4 utility trolleybus 408 stands outside Cleveland Road depot prior to working the NTA tour of 5 April 1964. An off-duty tower wagon stands outside the depot offices. *John Hughes collection*

Opposite middle: Whilst on the 5 April 1964 tour 408 attempted (unsuccessfully, as the power was off) to work the Chubb Street loop as part of the trip. The driver is seen here holding the trolleybus back, having just cleared the points to test for live current; the booms are being transferred back to the 'main line' to continue through Victoria Square. *John Hughes collection*

Opposite bottom: As part of the tour the Great Bridge Road loop was covered on the run from Darlaston, by the simple expedient of de-poling and using enthusiast power to push the trolley around the corner, whereupon the booms were reunited with the wiring in Great Bridge Road. *John Hughes collection*

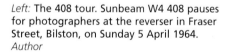

Above: During the tour the opportunity was taken to pose 408 on the Green Dragon loop. Here it is being passed by service trolley 646, with white steering wheel, denoting an 8ft-wide vehicle, clearly visible. *John Hughes collection*

Left: The 408 tour. Sunbeam W4 408 pauses for photographers at the reverser in Fraser Street, Bilston, on Sunday 5 April 1964. *Author*

Left: Midway through the tour, 408 enters Cleveland Road depot for a layover. *Author*

Above: Rounding the west–south spur at Fighting Cocks, on the way to Dudley. NTA Secretary David Smith stands on the platform, having just pulled the cord operating the manual point. *Author*

Above: Back at Fighting Cocks on the return run from Dudley, 408 has stopped in the through wiring bay alongside Guy BT 651 on a local working. *Author*

In May the decision was taken that no further Park Royal-bodied trolleys were to be repainted. During the same month overhead equipment was steadily being removed from the Amos Lane and Merryhill routes.

By July a further 15 replacement motor buses were on order for delivery in 1965, while all the redundant trolleybuses at Park Lane depot had been disposed of to Bricklin's scrapyard at Dudley Fields, Walsall.

The Walsall route was to see more problems on 7 July, when an explosion in electrical ducting blew off a manhole cover, damaging brickwork and leaving the electrical supply severed to route 29 at the Walsall end of the line, Walsall Corporation trolleybus services to Beechdale Estate and Bloxwich also being unable to operate. Motor buses were drafted in to cover until the power supply was re-connected.

Queen Square traffic was disrupted on 8 July when a trolleybus became disabled after a brass collector head became detached and fell to the ground, a female pedestrian suffering a laceration to the head and concussion. A Transport Department spokesman stated that it was a most unusual incident and could not understand how such an item could come loose. The pedestrian was taken to hospital and later made a full recovery. Learner drivers were still being trained continuously, even with trolleybuses being withdrawn, to cover the rapid turnover in staff, five trainee vehicles being noted on the Whitmore Reans–Darlaston service in one day.

During the summer it was announced that, in connection with British Rail's forthcoming electrification programme for the area, the Waterglade railway bridge at the Willenhall end of route 25 would be closed in early November, thereby severing the service. Inevitably this became the next casualty to be placed on the abandonment list. Delivery of the motor buses that were required for the conversion had already been delayed by strikes, and it was agreed that, should they not arrive on time, a temporary turning-circle would be constructed adjacent to the railway bridge, with passengers expected to walk the last quarter of a mile into Willenhall. It can safely be assumed that, had it already been a motorbus service, the Council would have provided an alternative route into Willenhall for the passengers' convenience. In the event it was not to be, and Birmingham buses were again hired in, the cost being met by British Rail.

The route was to see an interruption of service on 22 August, when trolley 436 became de-wired midway between Bilston and Fighting Cocks, badly bending a collector head in the process. Some way further along the route wooden spacing bars had again failed, the wiring being several feet apart for 100 yards. It was not to be a good day for drivers on this route. Minor roadworks the following day on the Wolverhampton–Bilston section ably demonstrated the ability of a trolleybus to move to the far side of the carriageway, underneath the opposite set of wires, without problem if driven with care.

Services to Sedgley and Dudley experienced their own problems at mid-day on 26 August, when power failed in the section beyond Fighting Cocks on Gibbons Hill. Drivers of trolleybuses returning from Sedgley were unaware of the problems ahead and, once in the dead section, coasted down the hill to form a growing queue of stranded vehicles within sight of the Fighting Cocks loop. Power was restored to the section at 2.45pm, a procession of trolleys making their way to Snow Hill. One of the more notorious trolleys was 428. An extremely sluggish vehicle at the best of times, it was still to be seen in service, plying its leisurely trade, and could often be found on the Dudley route with the following trolleys within sight and closing on it.

On Saturday 29 August Bilston depot found itself in a tight position for trolleybuses as a result of unusually high demand on route 25, and a request to Cleveland Road depot for help saw two trolleys

Above: Horseley Fields on the night of 26 April 1964. A wooden spacing bar had failed around 8.30pm, and, with queues building up, the repair wagon was soon on the scene, an inspector directing alternate trolleys around the problem by means of wrong-wire working, to ensure a flow of trolleys on this important route. *Author*

despatched via route 47 to assist. Monday 31st saw the first-ever August Bank Holiday specials between Dudley and Sedgeley, owing to exceptional crowds in Wolverhampton wanting to travel to Dudley Zoo. The first special had arrived from Wolverhampton at 10.47am, and under the jurisdiction of an inspector in Sedgley and another at Dudley a half-hourly shuttle service commenced. It was joined by a sister vehicle in the afternoon, increasing the frequency to 15 minutes. Operation of the specials ensured that people living further out along the route could board a trolleybus.

Demolition on the Wednesfield route was now well advanced, wiring at the Elephant & Castle junction of Cannock Road and Lower Stafford Street being removed. A fares increase and the abolition of through fares on cross-town routes, which measures had been proposed the

previous month, came into force on 21 September.

Failure of the Great Bridge Road frog on 3 October saw 440 in difficulties on a Darlaston working, as one trolley boom diverged when passing under the pointwork.

Suspension of cross-country route 25 finally came on 25 October 1964. As expected, the bridge construction works had brought forward the closure date. In an attempt to stave off his employer's blind determination to abandon the trolleys on the weak precept of roadworks, Eric Ball, who was in charge of overhead equipment, had put forward an economic proposal for an easily and quickly built turning-circle just short of the doomed Waterglade railway bridge, on available waste ground and using traction poles and wire retained from earlier abandonments, but this was overruled without any consideration being

given to the idea. With enthusiasts out in force, a last journey had been made on 440 at 11pm from Bilston to Fighting Cocks and back. As the trolley arrived outside Bilston depot the overhead pointwork was forgotten in the drama of the event, and it was left to the author to make a hasty exit from the platform of the still-moving vehicle and operate the manual frog by means of a hand cord attached to a traction pole adjacent to the depot entrance, thus ensuring the trolley booms did not make a last-minute bid for freedom in the direction of Willenhall. No 440 then entered Bilston depot for the last time, coming to a gentle halt in the middle of the depot yard. Final duties on the Willenhall section were performed by No 428.

After what amounted to 34 years of trolleybus operation since the route opened, Birmingham Corporation buses were again hired in, this time of the Daimler CVD6 type and working out of Cleveland Road depot. Interestingly, closure of the trolleybus service was officially confirmed only on 8 February 1965, when Wolverhampton Corporation recommenced operation with new 72-seat motor buses, once more working out of Bilston depot alongside the remaining trolleybuses servicing route 47. As a result of the conversion eight trolleybuses were withdrawn, although three were subsequently reassigned as training vehicles and moved to Cleveland Road depot.

Overhead repairmen were again in action on 14 November, attending to failed wiring in Victoria Square. This resulted in queues of trolleybuses, wreaking inevitable havoc with road traffic.

Christmas 1964 saw additional traffic arrangements on the Dudley Road routes, including a 6.59am working on Christmas Eve to the Green Dragon and extra workings on service 61 to Sedgley at 6.52am, 7.27am, 8.5am and 10.15pm.

Icy conditions at 6.40am on the morning of 15 January resulted in the driver of a Dudley-bound trolleybus losing control and entering the garden of 5 Dudding Road, via the front gate and hedge. Fortunately no serious damage was sustained by either the property or trolleybus. Another hold-up occurred on 22 January when a skate, weighing some 7lb, became detached from a Whitmore Reans-bound trolley swinging wide of badly parked cars. One trolley boom left the running wires, bringing down support and tensioning wires, the section feeder simultaneously shutting off power, and some time elapsed before all wiring was corrected and power restored.

By now all redundant wiring had been removed from the town centre. February saw yet another breakdown on the 24th, this time at Snow Hill, when (under an inspector's guidance) inbound trolleys had to de-pole, in the middle of a set of traffic lights, short of a broken wire, and coast down to their terminus outside C&A's store.

In March prewar Guy trolleybuses 277 and 280 were sent to Ferromet's scrapyard on the Bilston Road, having been used as mobile polling booths for a number of years following withdrawal. Repaints included 439 and 455, while an unusual step was taken in that 478's rear end was completely rebuilt. A complete overhaul was also given to 444, which had earned a bad reputation with crews as a slow runner with a poor top speed. When in service it would, after two or three trips, be falling well behind schedule, with at least one other trolley right behind. Once overhauled, its poor running rectified, it was outstationed at Bilston depot for the rest of its service life.

Wiring had now gone from Bradmore crossroads and was being removed from route 25 between Bilston and Ettingshall railway bridge.

The early part of the month saw a severe snowfall during the evening of the 3rd, grit and salt being issued and stowed in the stairwell of all service trolleys. Vehicle insulation was inevitably affected by the damp and slushy conditions, and in the days that followed up to 20 trolleys returned to the depot at any one time to dry out. Later that month, on the night of the 27th, power was turned off whilst No 1 rectifier at Commercial Road power station was extensively cleaned and overhauled by the Electricity Board. Meanwhile 16 March witnessed a long queue of trolleybuses at Fighting Cocks, following yet another power failure on the climb up Gibbons Hill to Sedgley. On 31 March there was a

Above: The 455 tour, Sunday 11 April 1965. Immaculately turned-out Sunbeam W4/Roe 455 waits in Victoria Square, underneath the famous clock (since relocated to the Black Country Living Museum), for the 1pm start. *Author*

particularly unwelcome peak-hour de-wirement at the Great Bridge Road junction, the tower wagon parking in the middle of the intersection while 416 and 417 cautiously negotiated their way through the frogs, ably demonstrating the ability of the trolleybus to deviate some distance from the 'centre line' when required.

On Sunday 4 April roadworks commenced at the town end of Snow Hill. This, once again, involved the coasting of trolleybuses on inward journeys, those coming into service from the depot in Cleveland Road having a difficult time of it.

Once again the annual NTA tour drew near, and on Sunday 11 April Roe-bodied trolleybus 455 left Cleveland Road depot at 12.50pm for Victoria Square, from where the tour started shortly after 1pm, covering all sections still workable, including Whitmore Reans (via route 2), Darlaston, Bilston depot, the Great Bridge Road loop (unauthorised but done nevertheless), Dudley (with all its short-working permutations) and Walsall. The still wired-up and energised section of abandoned route 25 from Fighting Cocks traffic lights to Goldthorn Hill terminus was covered by manually pushing 455 around the corner on arrival from Dudley and re-connecting to the overhead. Included in the tour was a short trip on Guy Wulfrunian 71 over abandoned routes 4, 9, 12, 13 and 32, possibly the first ever 'trolleybus' tour on the latter route! The day finished with 455 arriving back in Victoria Square at 6.30pm.

The following Friday a Roe-bodied trolley disgraced itself by de-wiring whilst turning around the difficult Green Dragon circle at 5.30pm, the situation not being helped by the peak-hour traffic. The previous evening had seen overhead fittings failing again, wiring descending into Victoria Square, but this time it was quickly repaired.

In May Walsall was announced as the next route for closure, although the trolleybuses themselves were not scheduled to come off until September. However, all services on the route were temporarily halted by a bad accident on Saturday 26 June, when a freak high wind caused Walsall 354, an ex-Ipswich vehicle, to overturn whilst passing Bentley Estate on its way to Wolverhampton. Regretfully this

Above: Sunbeam W4 411 returns to Cleveland Road depot to dry out after suffering a breakdown in vehicle insulation in the damp, slushy conditions. When this occurred passengers would often experience a mild electric shock when touching metal parts as they boarded or alighted. *Author's collection*

Above: A crash occurred on the Walsall route at Bentley on Saturday 26 June 1965 involving Walsall Corporation 354, an ex-Ipswich vehicle, which toppled over, fatally injuring a pedestrian. The trolley is shown after righting by breakdown crews. *Author's collection*

Above: A queue of Walsall-bound trolleys working 'wrong line' on the overhead wait to pass the stricken 354. *Author's collection*

was to prove fatal for one person, crushed when the trolley toppled onto the pavement. A fleet of ambulances took the 13 injured passengers to hospital as firemen, police and transport officials dealt with the removal of the damaged trolleybus. A queue of trolleys built up either side of the accident, and single-line running was put into operation, using 'wrong line' working for Walsall-bound vehicles, due to the position of 354 after (according to the driver's statement) the wind had blown it to the far side of the road.

The summer of 1965 saw the reintroduction of Saturday special workings, in the form of three afternoon runs to Dudley, two from Bilston and one from Wolverhampton via Bilston, the west–south spur at Fighting Cocks proving its worth once more. Three evening workings from Bilston to Dudley also ran, between 5pm and 5.30.

An unexpected announcement in July decreed that the Whitmore Reans–Darlaston service, rather than that to Walsall, would be the next to be withdrawn, in August, due partly to the fact that much of the overhead equipment on this route was fairly new and would be used to replace ageing fittings on the Dudley route.

The Indian summer of 1965 saw exceptionally heavy weekend traffic to Dudley, many people taking advantage of the fine weather to visit Dudley Zoo. In such circumstances all available trolleys were turned out. On several occasions '402' utilities 408, 409 and 413 were observed putting up spirited performances along the high Burton Road stretch, acquitting themselves in grand style, in what was now the autumn of their lives.

On Monday 9 August the 24-hour clock was introduced within the Transport Department and applied to all timetables. From the same date motor buses took over as planned on routes 2, 7 and 47, and as a result 14 trolleybuses were withdrawn from service. This ended operation of Guy trolleybuses in England and also saw the final demise of Bilston depot for trolleybus operation, 433 being the last trolleybus to enter service from the depot, at 2.10pm on the Sunday. (The depot would linger on, providing some motor-bus cover for the Darlaston services, until 23 January 1967, after which it was responsible for workings on route 25 only.) This closure also saw the end of a long-established procedure whereby an inspector stood each night under Victoria Square clock, whistle in hand, ready to signal the 11pm departure to all trolleybuses waiting in adjacent side streets. It was not unknown for several trolleys to move off simultaneously, creating an inevitable power surge, resulting in a double thump of sound from the cab as the circuit-breakers tripped, dimming the saloon lights momentarily, until the handles were re-set by the driver.

As will be apparent from the unfolding scenario, the Transport Department had, on instructions issued by the Council many months previously, reduced maintenance to the basic minimum consistent with safety; the fact that this gave the trolleybus system a bad public image, with continual failures both of vehicles and of overhead fittings, did not appear to bother the corporate conscience of Council members.

Trolleybus 478 was in trouble on 11 August, when it failed midway between Fighting Cocks and Wolverhampton, 408 failing simultaneously at the top of Gibbons Hill, while an accident on the 24th saw 415 withdrawn from the 29 service. Garrick Street then became the focus of unwelcome attention at 10.30am on 29 September, when the pointwork and support wiring at the Cleveland Road turn was dislodged, becoming unsafe for road users underneath. Traffic quickly built up, a queue of returning trolleys being unable to proceed to either Cleveland Road depot or Dudley and having to be held in line alongside the Savoy cinema in Garrick Street until repairs were complete.

By now the active fleet had been reduced to just 40 vehicles, of which 12

Above: The Indian summer of 1965, with the Sunbeam W4 utility class putting up 'a spirited performance in the autumn of their lives' on the high Burton Road stretch. *Author*

Above: Sunbeam 413 stands on the cobbles at the waiting area in Stone Street while the duty inspector chats with crew in the summer of 1965. *Author*

more were due to be withdrawn on 31 October, when trolleybuses ceased running on the Willenhall–Walsall service. Several had been moved during the day in readiness for the abandonment, as the Sunday schedule required only two or three vehicles from each operator. It was a cold and wet night when the end came for routes 5 and 29. As 10.30pm approached, groups of people — enthusiasts and well-wishers alike — began to arrive at St James Square, to the bemusement of local residents, flashlight photography being used to record the last departures. Following on the heels of the final service departure, 446 left St James Square at 10.34pm on a specially organised round-trip for NTA members, although one late-night reveller in Willenhall, having missed the last service trolleybus got an unexpected free ride to Walsall! The last service trolleybus on route 5 was 432 from Wolverhampton and Willenhall, the last trolleys on the 29 being 434 (from Walsall) and Walsall Corporation 353 (from Wolverhampton).

Conversion of routes 5 and 29 brought to an end the unique example of joint trolleybus operation (with Walsall Corporation), which had spanned almost 37 years. As was the case with most conversions, the new motor buses operated on a reduced frequency due to their increased seating capacity — small comfort to passengers waiting in the wind and rain, bemoaning the loss of a once-frequent trolleybus service. In a little under 17 months the remnants of a once impressive trolleybus system would be just a memory.

By now overhead fittings had been removed from part of the route to Bilston and also in the Mount Pleasant area, the repair bay at Cleveland Road being stripped out at the same time. By 4 November the Willenhall turning-circle had also disappeared. Icy weather on

Above: Sunbeam W4 408 in trouble on the climb to Sedgley during the evening rush hour on Wednesday 11 August 1965. It has failed just short of the summit and is being passed by a hastily organised replacement motor bus. *Author*

Above: The motor bus having passed, the crew of 408 took advantage of a lull in the traffic to push their charge back into a side street, where they awaited the arrival of the tow wagon. *Author*

Above: A tow wagon has now arrived to take 408 back to Cleveland Road depot for assessment and repair. Sadly the trolley was to be withdrawn just over two months later, on 31 October 1965. *Author*

Wednesday 24 November caused operating difficulties along the length of the Dudley route, severe problems being encountered near the Green Dragon circle in the Kent Street area; several trolleybuses came to a standstill, being unable to proceed along the hilly roads.

At the end of the year tower wagon No 8 was withdrawn after suffering damage under a low bridge. Removal of the negative wires on the Darlaston route was now complete, while a section of Transport Road wiring had also gone, as had the pointwork to the car shed at Cleveland Road depot from the Snow Hill direction.

Sedgley Bull Ring was at the centre of de-wirement problems at 8.30am on 18 January 1966, when a trolley on service 61 lost both booms from the wiring, the booms jamming at an angle against the pull-off wires; jams built up on roads feeding into the Bull Ring while the crew worked to get the poles re-connected, the trolleybus eventually moving off at 8.45am.

At a hearing on 23 March on the Transport Department's proposal for a fares increase, General Manager Mr R. H. Addlesee, M Inst T, M Inst TA, stated that, whilst it had been hoped to replace the remaining trolleybuses in September, delays in the delivery of new buses now made the change unlikely before December. However, the fares increase was granted, and the revised fares would take effect from 11 April.

Figures published for the financial year ending 31 March 1966 revealed that the active fleet averaged 117 miles daily, while 3,750,069 units of electricity had been consumed and £7,216 spent on removing redundant overhead equipment.

On 6 April the evening peak-hour service to Dudley was curtailed just short of the Blind School (properly the Wolverhampton & Dudley Institute for the Blind) at the foot of Gibbons Hill at approximately 6.40pm; again this was due to a sudden collapse of wiring, consistent with the minimum standard of maintenance that was now being carried out. The evening was to see further problems at 8pm, when 433 became stranded with a mechanical fault just short of Kent Street. The Green Dragon turning-circle was the scene of yet more chaos on 20 April, when a Roe-bodied vehicle on training duties mounted the pavement whilst attempting to negotiate the circle and became de-wired, causing considerable damage to both booms. The trolleybus was pushed back onto a nearby garage forecourt to await the arrival of the tower wagon, which towed it back in disgrace to Cleveland Road depot. Only six more days were to pass before a section of wiring at the Green Dragon detached and fell onto the carriageway, having almost certainly been

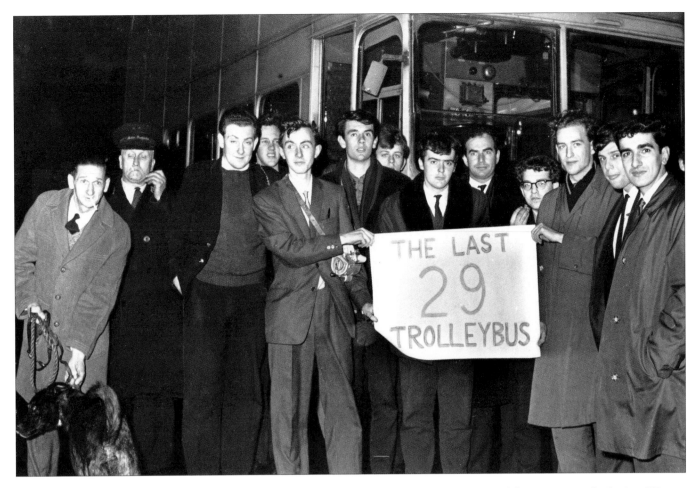

Above: The end of the road for joint trolleybus operation. Following the last service trip by 434 a special run was organised using 446, seen here on arrival at Townend Bank, Walsall, on 31 October 1965. This really was the last trolleybus on route 29, and the opportunity was taken to record the occasion for posterity. A youthful author is fourth from the left. *Author's collection*

loosened by the events of a few days earlier. After completing repairs at this location the overhead crew proceeded to Fighting Cocks, where they put in several new span wires for good measure.

Although most of the wiring between Wolverhampton and Willenhall had been removed, Walsall Corporation had by the spring of 1966 not removed any of its wiring, with the exception of a short stretch from the traffic island in the centre of Willenhall to the overhead boundary, plus the offending section where the new M6 motorway was crossed.

Sunday 22 May saw the annual NTA tour take place, but this time with a difference, using the first-ever preserved trolleybus, this being the NTA's own vehicle; Huddersfield 541 was a Sunbeam MS2 with 70-seat Park Royal bodywork, first registered in 1947 and withdrawn, after 17 years' continuous service, on 28 February 1964. For two weeks prior to the tour it was parked up, courtesy of the Transport Department, at the Oxford Street pound, where, in secure though open storage, NTA members carried out last-minute checks to the rear axle-grease boxes and touched up the paintwork as required. The tour was well patronised, and although there

remained only one route, to Dudley, every inch of available wiring was covered, including the full circle at Sedgley Bull Ring. However, this was not the first trolleybus tour of 1966, for at the beginning of the year the Manchester Trolleybus Preservation Society had organised a trip to Dudley, using 432.

Below: The 541 tour, Sunday 22 May 1966. Preserved Huddersfield Sunbeam MS2 trolleybus 541, of 1947 vintage, moves cautiously out of Cleveland Road depot to commence the annual Wolverhampton trolleybus tour. *Author*

Above: Bilston Street, Wolverhampton. Huddersfield 541 stands behind service trolley 453 at the Dudley loading point. *Author*

During the evening of 31 July, whilst passing the Blind School, Dudley-bound 439 caught up with and collided with the rear of 429. Little damage was caused to either vehicle, apart from some slight bending of the trolley booms, and after some remedial work by an overhead crew both the trolleybuses were allowed to proceed.

During the last week of October an experimental one-way traffic system at the town end of the Dudley route necessitated the slewing of the outbound wires to the far side of the road. Eventually they were returned to their normal position, but the surplus fittings used were left in place in the span wiring.

On Sunday 20 November the Corporation granted the NTA permission to test-run to Dudley with Rotherham 44, its preserved blue three-axle trolleybus, which had arrived at Cleveland Road depot the previous day. Having reached the Stone Street turning area it stood in company with service trolleys while undergoing a brief mechanical check. All appeared well, and 44 then set off back to Wolverhampton, slotted in between the regular workings. There were no hitches with the run, and 44 put in a spirited performance climbing Gibbons Hill, where it attracted several stares from local people.

With effect from 6 January 1967 the town loading point for route 58 was moved from Bilston Street around the cor-

ner to what had previously been used as the unloading stop outside the C&A shop. The re-siting was brought about by road works in Bilston Street that occupied two thirds of the carriageway, causing a bottle-neck at the previous loading point.

Despite having only one basic route left and being committed to full closure, the trolleybus system in Wolverhampton still

held the title for the highest-frequency service in daily operation in the British Isles: at peak times the operation of routes 8, 58 and 61 combined to offer an impressive 2½-minute headway between Wolverhampton and Fighting Cocks, and it was said that there was always a trolley-bus in sight on the stretch to the Fighting Cocks turning-circle.

Above: Traffic congestion in Dudley Street, Sedgley, as 541 joins two Roe-bodied Sunbeams on service workings. *Author*

7. Final Act

News broke in January that Sunday 5 March 1967 would be the last day of trolleybus operation in Wolverhampton, with mixed motor-bus working, while the previous day would see the last day of full trolleybus service. With the inevitable dismay felt for a battle lost came a sense of urgency to 'do the right thing' and see the trolleybuses out in a manner befitting their loyal contribution to the town. Wolverhampton Corporation declared, unsurprisingly, that no special events or services would be laid on to commemorate the passing of the trolleybuses, and it fell to the NTA and other enthusiast groups to bring forward plans for a special farewell tour, determined efforts behind the scenes

finally bearing fruit and persuading a reluctant Corporation to agree to the proposed events.

The first signs of preparation came on the morning of 11 February, when a policeman on traffic duty in Princes Square was caught unawares as Guy BT 654 appeared on tow, coming up Stafford Street towards him. With great presence of mind he quickly stepped forward and, raising his hand to stop the traffic in Lichfield Street, waved the convoy through on its way to Cleveland Road depot. There 654 was given a thorough clean and overhaul followed by a repaint complete with grey roof — all courtesy of the Corporation — and the following day was successfully tested on a run to Dudley

and back. A few days later Rotherham 44 came in for a similar check-up.

Contemporaneously with the impending abandonment British Rail's London Midland Region had for some months been preparing for electrification of the railway line between Wolverhampton (High Level) and London (Euston) with the intention of starting the new service on Monday 6 March. Part of the argument put forward in the press for conversion from diesel to electric haulage was that the new service would be cleaner, quicker, more efficient and cheaper. The irony was not lost on the townspeople of Wolverhampton, when, in the weeks leading up to closure, the Council presented a similar case, in an effort to press home its argument for conversion from electric trolleybuses to diesel motor buses. Virtually identical, one of the arguments had to be flawed, and history has shown that in this case the railway had got it right. Sadly, but somewhat inevitably, the Council had got it wrong yet again.

The weeks leading up to March were a hive of activity as the NTA compiled a schedule of events for the last weekend. This was rapidly put together and co-ordinated with the various official bodies and preservation groups. Many photographers were in evidence on Saturday the 4th, recording every aspect of what would now be the last day of full trolleybus service, their efforts continuing unabated into the hours of darkness.

Above; On a misty morning Rotherham 44 arrives at Dudley on a test run to ensure its mechanical and electrical fitness, prior to the grand tour on the last weekend. *Author*

Right: Stone Street, Dudley, on Saturday 4 March 1967. Sunbeam 435 prepares to leave as photographers busy themselves recording the scene for posterity.
John Hughes collection

Above: **Professional to the end, a smartly dressed Amy Roberts stands by her charge, 437, in Stone Street, Dudley, on Saturday 4 March 1967.** *John Hughes collection*

Left: On the last Saturday of operation, 4 March 1967, Sunbeam/Roe trolleys including 432 and 435 are seen working the ever-busy section at Fighting Cocks, their drivers determined to go out in style. *Author*

Right: The scene at Cleveland Road early on the morning of Sunday 5 March 1967. Six of the trolleybuses that were to work the last day's service — 447, 448, 444, 449, 446 and 455 — are already lined up outside the depot. *Author*

Left: The view towards Snow Hill on the morning of Sunday 5 March 1967 as the six trolleys destined to work the last day's services silently await their respective departure times. *Author*

Unknown to many present that Saturday evening, a lone trolleybus had slipped quietly down Cleveland Road following the last public departure from Snow Hill and made two round trips of the route to Dudley. This had been hired by the Maypine Trolleybus Co (based in Great Bookham, Surrey), which owned and operated a 1/3-scale model trolleybus system in private grounds, the vehicles using ex-milk-float chassis and motors, with hand-built replica bodies. Maypine owner Mr P. H. Lepine-Smith, in possession of a full Group 8 licence, was at the wheel of the trolleybus and was joined by a small group of friends for the trip.

Sunday dawned quietly, with a grey and lifeless sky. In time the sun began to rise gently behind Cleveland Road depot, the dew still fresh upon the green woodwork of the doors, as they were pulled open to release trolleybuses into service. The first of the trolleys then backed out across Cleveland Road, as they had done for so many years, to the annoyance of the Ministry of Transport, to take up the 7.15am working. As early as 8am little knots of people, some of them members of the NTA, from as far away as Glasgow and Maidstone, had begun to assemble outside the depot. Preserved motor buses also began to arrive, bringing in more enthusiasts. The trolleys that were to operate the final day's service — 444/6-9/51/2/5 — were lined up, as always, at the kerbside; they, at least, had one day left, but for those still within the depot or stranded elsewhere on the erstwhile system there was no future.

At 9am the cortège started as 424-7/9/35/7-40/53/4 were dragged away to scrapyards on the Bilston Road, where they joined 441, withdrawn previously. Five years ago the paint on their then new Roe

bodies had gleamed; now each was to be reduced to eight tons of scrap. Back in the depot the new motor buses had taken up most of the available room.

The two tour trolleybuses were brought out and parked in the line of town-facing vehicles, and at 10.30am prompt the final grand tour commenced, with Rotherham 44 in the lead, closely followed by Wolverhampton Guy BT 654, with Driver Peter McKloskey at the wheel and Inspector Howard Davies supervising the event, the departure being filmed by BBC Television. After passing through Snow Hill and Fighting Cocks in bright sunshine the two trolleybuses stormed their way up the hill to Sedgley and continued in convoy on the six-mile run through to Dudley, where a lengthy photographic stop was made in the Stone Street turning bay. A service trolley was already there, and as another made its way in along Priory Street it created a busy

spectacle reminiscent of times past. The whole scene was atmospheric and heavy with nostalgia. It was hard to believe that in 24 hours this would all be history! A run back to Wolverhampton then followed, both trolleys heading up Cleveland Road to be parked outside the depot whilst the intermediate part of the tour came into operation. This consisted of a hired Midland Red D9 bus, which proceeded to traverse various abandoned parts of the trolleybus system, including Walsall. Some tour passengers remained behind at the depot to patronise the NTA sales stand, an ex-Rotherham Corporation Bristol motor bus converted to a tower wagon, which was selling souvenirs almost as quickly as the official 'wrecking party' could retrieve them from the nearby scrapyard on Bilston Road.

During the morning 433, with Driver Lol Williams at the wheel, joined the fray at 10.15am, working a privately chartered

Above: Rotherham 44 and Wolverhampton 654 stand together in Cleveland Road ready to start the grand final tour. *Author*

Above: Having arrived in Dudley, the tour trolleys stand in line at the Stone Street terminus, their bodywork in pristine condition. *Author*

trip organised by the Wolverhampton Trolleybus Group for a full tour of the Dudley route and taking in such places as the circle of wiring at Sedgley Bull Ring. Stops were made at several locations to enable a photographic record to be made of the event. After the tour 433 was towed direct to Bilston depot for safe storage prior to preservation and joined sister trolley 432, which had been taken there during the morning. By now the full quota of eight service vehicles was running, including 446, which, by special arrangement, had been allocated to operate the last journey of all.

The tour proper recommenced at 1.27pm with journeys by Rotherham 44 covering the short workings at Fighting Cocks and the Green Dragon, this vehicle, perhaps inappropriately, becoming the last to use this particular wiring.

On return to Cleveland Road depot 44 was joined at 2.50pm by 654 for a ceremonial last trip to Dudley — then, as always, Worcestershire's only trolleybus terminus. For this journey the Deputy General Manager and Engineer, Mr D. P. Martin, joined those on board. A stop was made halfway up Gibbons Hill and within sight of Sedgley Beacon, at one of the few remaining points where a rural background could be provided, and many photographs were taken, in brilliant sunshine, using a well-positioned air-raid shelter and an equally convenient grit bunker for standing on. Failures had reduced the quota of service vehicles to six and these continued to pass the two parked-up tour trolleys at regular intervals with trolley booms being removed from the wires as needed.

The trip also included the by then obligatory tour option of a one-and-a-half-times circle around the Bull Ring at Sedgley, thus ensuring that every piece of wiring was traversed. During this movement and the turning at the Green Dragon, which proved to be very tight for Rotherham 44, considerable disruption was caused as traffic queues built up. But, on this day of all days, nobody really seemed to care. Officially the last two trolleybus movements at these turning points involved Rotherham 44 at the Green Dragon and 654 (from Dudley) at Sedgley Bull Ring. The two trolleybuses then proceeded in convoy back to Cleveland Road depot, where the tour finished at 4pm, 44 and 654 then returning to the NTA storage site at Coven, north of Wolverhampton, to join two trolleys already preserved — Cardiff 243 and Huddersfield 541. Many participants then adjourned to the nearby Victoria Hotel for refreshments and, commandeering a television to see the results of the BBC presence at the start of the tour, were duly rewarded with 45 seconds of coverage on the national news bulletin.

Trolleybus 449 finished the last Fighting Cocks working, turning there at 1.39pm, after which motor buses took over for the rest of the day. It is ironic to note that, on being transferred to route 58 shortly afterwards, 449 broke down and refused to move. It was towed in together with 447, which had failed earlier in the day on a 58 working, joining its companions.

This was also to be a sad occasion for the last remaining lady driver, Amy Davies, in charge of 448 that day. Whilst women were permitted to drive trolleybuses, an anomaly in the law at that time did not allow them to drive PSVs, and with the final closure Amy would have to return to the ranks of 'clippies'. Thankfully this law has long since been amended to allow women to drive motor buses.

As late evening approached an atmosphere of sad resignation began to pervade the area, crowds gathering in Snow Hill as the allotted time drew near. Nos 455 and 452 coasted in down the hill, arriving on service workings and drew up outside C&A's store to unload. As the trolleys stopped, amidst the pop of flashlight photographs being taken, throngs of people surged forward to get a closer look. Having loaded up with as many of the burgeoning crowd as the duty inspector would permit, they pulled out, virtually in convoy, on their last revenue-earning duties.

Left: Guy BT 654 stands with Rotherham 44 in Stone Street, Dudley, during the final tour on Sunday 5 March 1967. *Author*

Right: In the bright afternoon sunshine 654 stands, gleaming and pristine, halfway up Gibbons Hill, with open countryside and the foot of Sedgley Beacon to the right. This was the ceremonial final run to Dudley. *Author*

Left: Rotherham 44 arrives to join Wolverhampton 654 on the last run to Dudley. Both trolleys were held here for several minutes, to the delight of photographers. *Author*

Above: A group photograph of Wolverhampton's lady trolleybus drivers. Amy Roberts, wearing glasses and sitting in the centre of the front row, was the town's last female driver, manning 437 on Saturday 4 March and 448 on Sunday 5 March, the last day of operation. *John Hughes collection*

Above: Wolverhampton's last female driver, Amy Davies, brings Sunbeam F4 626 into Garrick Street, past the Savoy cinema, at the start of a trip to Dudley. *Author's collection*

Above: Stone Street terminus in Dudley. Sunbeam 446 swings into the loading bay as enthusiasts and well-wishers capture the moment on film. *Author*

Minutes later, voices were raised amongst the onlookers and a ragged cheer went up as 446 was spotted coming down Snow Hill for what was to be the last pickup for the Dudley run. As it approached to a barrage of flashbulbs, the crowds surged forward, enveloping the trolleybus as it stopped. The Council, somewhat wary of public feeling and general resentment at the closure, had requested a Police presence. However, the turnout was largely good-natured, and the policemen on duty had little to do other than guide traffic around the mass of people spilling out across the road.

There was a scramble by enthusiasts and well-wishers alike, to board the vehicle, which, full with several standing passengers, saw some regular travellers to Sedgley left behind as 446 pulled out at 10.40pm. An inspector travelling on the rear platform was followed by a car containing more inspectors — it would seem that those in authority were determined to see the last vestiges of trolleybus operation away before anyone had second thoughts. The column of vehicles in the funeral procession lengthened as a police car swung in behind the bus inspectors' transport as 446 passed through the pointwork at Fighting Cocks, the few regular passengers getting off shortly afterwards.

The atmosphere aboard was subdued as people reminisced about better times, looking out for familiar sights and sounds as

they passed through Sedgley Bull Ring and again as 446 slowed down and the trolley heads clicked their way through the pointwork at the Green Dragon public house on the corner of Jews Lane, the lights flickering and dimming momentarily as they passed through the dead sections. All too soon they were in Dudley, as 446 travelled down

Priory Street and swung into the square at Stone Street, the tyres rumbling over the Market Place cobbles as it pulled in behind 452. The passengers, most of whom were enthusiasts of one sort or another, got off and, spreading themselves across the square, proceeded to take as many photographic records as they could, as little knots

Above: It is 11.02pm in Stone Street, Dudley, on the night of Sunday 5 March 1967. At 11.04pm 452 will depart for Wolverhampton, and 446 will draw forward to pick up its passengers for the last-ever trolleybus journey between the two towns. *Author*

of people stood chatting to each other. All of this was watched by a number of Dudley's police officers, who remained discreetly in the background. Thus the last public-service trolleybus ever to operate into Worcestershire was recorded on film.

All too soon, at 11.04pm, 452 departed, to be followed at 11.12pm by 446, the return journey being another filled with sadness prompted by the knowledge that the end was approaching. At Sedgley another trolleybus was glimpsed disappearing back to Wolverhampton. This turned out to be 444; it transpired that, notwithstanding the fact that motor buses had nominally taken over the bulk of the operation on service 61 to Sedgley from 10.30pm onwards, an extra trolley had been requisitioned at short notice to work a late, unannounced special to Sedgley at 11pm, catering for the travellers unable to board 446.

Leaving Sedgley, 446 continued to tail 444, whose lights could be seen a quarter of a mile distant, down Gibbons Hill and on towards Fighting Cocks, where the Police left the procession. One fare-paying passenger had actually boarded at Sedgley, and when he came to get off just past the Fighting Cocks traffic lights the inspector found that power to the bells had failed. NTA Secretary David Smith promptly produced a whistle, and a deafening blast brought the trolleybus to a stop. Amidst more than a few smiles two more blasts on the whistle brought the trolley back to life — a rare example of co-operation and one that (on this occasion, at least) was appreciated by all. A novel touch was also provided by passenger Cliff Brown, who handed out some well-produced black-bordered souvenir cards to his fellow passengers.

Snow Hill was deserted as 446 made its way quietly down through the streets and past the closed shops to draw up at the unloading point. Upon arrival no one showed any inclination to get off, and after some discussion with the General Manager (who was waiting at the terminus) it was agreed that passengers might remain on board as far as the depot, for a fare of 3d each. This everyone did, which did not exactly please the conductor, who was

Above: On the return journey to Wolverhampton there was a mood of quiet contemplation on board 446 as passengers reflected on the day's events and pondered the impending end of trolleybus operation. *Author*

already a tired man, although this was probably the only time that a trolleybus ever made a profit on a depot journey. As 446 made its way along Garrick Street and up Cleveland Road the last ticket ever to be purchased on a service trolleybus in Wolverhampton — a blue 1½d (No HL58305) — was issued to David Smith.

The wiring at Cleveland Road depot was encountered for the last time as, shortly after midnight, 446 came to a halt in the middle of the road, surrounded by an estimated crowd of 200 people, some of whom had come from as far away as Rochester and Rotherham. There was reluctance on the part of many to leave, and for once restrictions were relaxed and a blind eye was turned as people entered the depot area. With unseemly haste the booms were removed from the life-giving wires, and with a tower wagon attached to the front 446 disappeared into the gloom and into history, heading for Bilston depot and intended (though unfulfilled) preservation. For the other trolleybuses that had come out of service that weekend it was a quick death — a tow straight to the scrapyard. The five trolleys still inside the depot were reversed out, disconnected from the overhead and then 444/8/51/2/5 were

towed to a yard on Bilston Road, 451 being the last trolleybus to move under its own power. After nearly 44 years of trolleybus operation this, surely, was the most ruthless system closure of them all.

As the depot doors slammed shut on the trolleybus era in Wolverhampton one wondered whether this really was the end of electric public transport on the town's roads. This had been the quintessential system, operating in a variety of different environments from busy town-centre streets, through quiet tree-lined suburban roads and even venturing into the open countryside. It encompassed most of the layout and wiring variations that were peculiar to British trolleybus operation, becoming part of the accepted street furniture, with its omnipresence and visibly enduring nature. Within this lay part of the reason and mystique that made it so appealing to the general public. Air pollution and noise are two of our biggest urban problems, and the trolleybus conquered both. It must be only a matter of time before engineers develop even more efficient systems to replace the internal-combustion engine. It was a foolish man who on 5 March 1967 bade a final farewell to the electric bus, for it is too good a principle for that.

At half past midnight on the morning of Monday 6 March 1967 a 'finished with traction supply' message was sent to Commercial Road power station, the circuit-breaker switch was thrown in Cleveland Road depot, cutting power to the depot itself and the adjacent wiring in Cleveland Road, and the lights went out for the Wolverhampton trolleybus.

Requiesce in pace, old friend.
Your time will come again.

Final duties on the Wolverhampton trolleybus system

Last tuition trolleybus: 452 (2/2/67)

Last service trolley to leave depot under power: 452 (5/3/67)

Last trolley of all (on NTA tour) to leave depot under power during the day: Rotherham 44 (5/3/67)

Last trolleybus on service 8 to turn at Fighting Cocks: 449 (1.39pm, 5/3/67)

Last trolley of all to turn at Fighting Cocks: Rotherham 44 (5/3/67)

Last timetabled trolley from Wolverhampton turning at Sedgley Bull Ring: 451 (11.14pm, 5/3/67)

Last trolley from Dudley (on NTA tour) to turn at Sedgley Bull Ring: 654 (5/3/67)

Last service trolley to turn at the Green Dragon: 444 (12.46pm, 4/3/67)

Last trolley of all to turn at the Green Dragon: Rotherham 44 (5/3/67)

Last trolley of all to leave depot under power: 451 (5/3/67)

Above: The end of the line. People mill about in the entrance to Cleveland Road depot after the arrival of 446, knowing it is all over but feeling lost and not wanting to leave the scene. In the next few minutes the remaining five trolleys, 444, 448, 451, 452 and 455, will be reversed out of the depot for the last time and towed away to the scrapyard; 451 will be the last to move under power. *Author*

In Affectionate Remembrance

of the

Wolverhampton Trolleybuses

| Which succumbed to the effects OF DIESEL FUMES ! | SUNDAY, MARCH 5th, 1967 |

After many years of faithful service

Modern Photo Litho Services (W'ton) Ltd.   42.

Postscript

The first replacement motor bus on Monday 6 March was No 80, a Guy with Metro-Cammell bodywork. It may be of little comfort (but surely some amusement) to know that, on entering service at 4.40am, ex Bilston Street for Dudley, it moved just twenty yards into Garrick Street before colliding with a car and was towed back to the depot in disgrace, having not even left Wolverhampton!

Appendices

Appendix I   Trolleybus Routes and Services

Number(s)	Route	Operational	Notes	Last service trolley
1	Tettenhall	29/11/27-30/06/63		622
2/7	Whitmore Reans–Darlaston (cross-town via Bilston)	27/01/30-08/08/65	A, B	(Whitmore Reans) 422 (Bilston) 440 (Darlaston) 446
3	Bushbury Hill–Fordhouses (cross-town service)	09/03/25-26/01/64	A, C	(Bushbury Hill) 439 (Fordhouses) 448
4	Penn Fields	11/07/27-09/06/63		498
5	Willenhall	16/05/27-31/10/65	D	432
6	Wednesfield	29/10/23-03/11/63	E	
8	Fighting Cocks	26/10/25-05/03/67		449
9 (88)	Jeffcock Road–Amos Lane (cross-town service)	21/03/32-29/09/63 and (88) 03/11/63	F	(Jeffcock Road) 423 (Amos Lane) 451
11	Penn	10/10/32-09/06/63		606
12	Finchfield–Low Hill (cross-town service)	10/04/33-03/11/63	A, F	444
13	Merry Hill–Low Hill (cross-town service)	10/04/33-03/11/63	A, F	616
25	Willenhall–Fighting Cocks (cross-country via Bilston)	27/10/30-25/10/64	A	(Willenhall) 428 (Fighting Cocks) 440
29	Walsall (jointly with Walsall Corporation)	16/11/31-31/10/65		434 (Walsall Corporation: 353)
32	Oxbarn Avenue	12/02/34-21/01/61		652
47	Bilston (Great Bridge Road)	24/10/49-08/08/65	A	409 (Fraser Street) 440
58	Dudley	08/07/27-05/03/67	A	446 (Green Dragon) 444
59	Wednesfield (The Albion)	10/01/55-03/11/63	E	446
61	Sedgley	10/11/26-05/03/67	G	451

Notes:

A   Peak-hour short workings generally used the main route number

B   Opening dates: Wolverhampton–Bilston 19/11/28
    Bilston–Darlaston 27/5/29
    Whitmore Reans–Darlaston 27/1/30

C   Opening dates: Wolverhampton to Fordhouses 9/3/25
    Wolverhampton to Bushbury Hill 30/11/31
    Fordhouses–Bushbury Hill 10/5/37

D   Opening dates: Wolverhampton–Willenhall (Neachells Lane) 16/5/27
    Neachells Lane–Market Place 16/9/27

E   When extended to Wood End was initially alternate working with service 59 but reverted to peak-hour-only in later years

    Opening dates: Wolverhampton–Wednesfield (Dog & Partridge) 29/10/23
    Wednesfield (Dog & Partridge)–Wood End 10/2/34
    Wood End–The Albion 10/1/55

F   When the Jeffcock Road section was abandoned the remaining part of the route to Amos Lane operated for a further five weeks as service 88

    Opening dates: Wolverhampton–Low Hill 21/3/32
    Amos Lane–Bradmore 21/3/32
    Merry Hill/Finchfield–Low Hill 10/4/33
    Wolverhampton–Jeffcock Road 8/11/37
    Amos Lane–Finchfield 8/11/37
    Jeffcock Road–Amos Lane 13/5/46
    Finchfield–Low Hill 13/5/46

G   When extended to Dudley was initially alternate working with service 58 but reverted to peak-hour-only in later years

Appendix II Tickets

After many years of use with Bell Punch equipment, inherited from the days of tramway operation, the 'Ultimate' system was adopted from the same manufacturer and its machines used, probably from the early 1950s. The tickets were a little more than half the size of the Bell Punch type, being colour coded and pre-printed with the fare and serial number.

The standard machine held five separate rolls, each containing 500 tickets. These were issued by depressing levers on the front of the machine. Four mechanical counters on the machine front recorded double-issue tickets, the fifth counter showing the total number of tickets sold, such information being recorded by the conductor on his trip sheet. It was important to remember what value was on each roll when issuing tickets to passengers. It was common practice for conductors to take the opportunity of opening the machine during quiet moments at the terminus, to check that they were not about to run out of a particular ticket roll halfway through a journey — changing rolls on a moving vehicle full of passengers was never easy and was to be avoided if at all possible.

In later days, machines were usually stocked with the following:

Grey	1½d
Green	2d
Pink	2½d
Purple	3d
White	6d

A number of six-roll machines were also in use and would additionally use one of the tickets shown below. These were printed on an occasional basis, to cover specific demands e.g. factory workers' travel.

Green	3½d	(overprinted with value)
Buff	4d	
Buff	4½d	
Pink	5d	(occasionally overprinted with value)

When the concessionary fares were introduced for elderly people, the 2d ticket was generally taken out to make way for them. They were:

Pale Yellow 1d   (overprinted with red 'S')

The early penny ticket was also yellow in colour but had been out of use for many years with the inevitable increases in fares charged.

Appendix III Overhead Equipment

Power station
Commercial Road — two 750kW Mercury Arc Rectifiers and one standby rotary converter

Feeder station
At half-mile intervals with heavy-duty cables to running wires

Current supply
550V DC

Substations

Bilston depot	750kW
Birches Barn (Barn Green)	500kW
Deans Road (Willenhall Road end)	400kW
Dudley (Eve Hill)	400kW
Fighting Cocks (side of 317 Dudley Road)	400kW
Heath Town, Coronation Road	400kW
Park Lane (at side of cold stores)	750kW
Sedgley (old depot)	750kW
Stafford Road (Goodyear's)	400kW
Wells Road (Penn)	400kW

Triangles
Whilst Wolverhampton did not indulge in the luxury of reverse loops, which were popular in Belfast, or interlaced points, as found on the Bradford and Cardiff systems, substantial use was made of that epitome of British trolleybus operation, the reversing triangle and these could be found at several locations across the system.

Route	Location
1	Wrottesley Road, Tettenhall Green (replaced in time by a turning circle)
7	Stowheath Lane (removed at an early date)
7	Bilston, Walsall Street (removed when replaced by Fraser Street)
47	Bilston, Fraser Street
9	Amos Lane (removed when service extended to 'The Pheasant')
9	Victoria Road, Fallings Park (discontinued at an early date)
9	Jeffcock Road, terminus at Downham Place
12	Finchfield, terminus at Coppice Road
12	Bradmore (removed after World War 2)

Emergency wiring
Emergency wiring was also in place to cover breakdowns and diversions, being strategically located at several points around the system. In some cases this was a throwback from earlier routes since diverted or closed. With the exception of Lower Stafford Street all wiring was tied off to the nearest traction pole and not connected physically — only electrically — to the rest of the system.

Bilston Street (between Garrick Street and Pipers Row)
Waterloo Road (between Newhampton Road East and Dunkley Street)
Lower Stafford Street (between Stafford Street and Stafford Road)
Stubbs Road (between Lea Road and Penn Road)
Thorneycroft Lane/Bushbury Road (east to north around the junction)

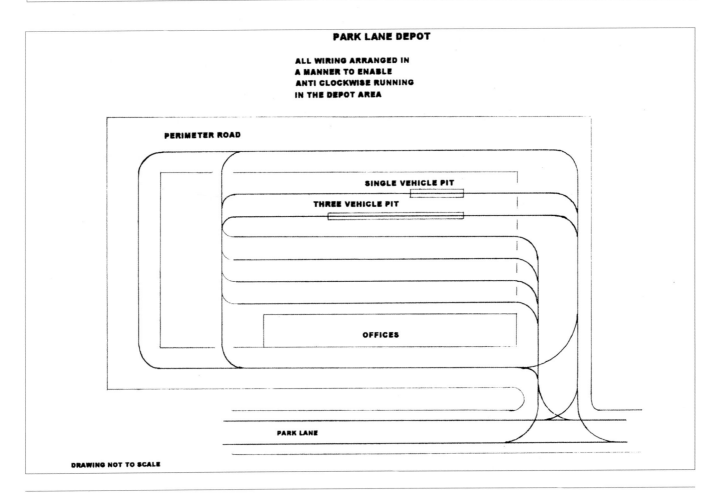

CLEVELAND ROAD DEPOT

FIGURES INDICATE ROWS OF
TROLLEYBUSES IN EACH BAY

EACH ROW HOLDS UP TO
5 TROLLEYS NOSE TO TAIL

SOME ROWS SHARE OVERHEAD WIRING

4   4   3   5   3

TRANSPORT ROAD

OFFICES

TOP SHED

WORKSHOP

CAR SHED

REPAIR BAY

MAIN SHED

NEWMARKET BAY

HOSPITAL STREET

VICARAGE ROAD

CLEVELAND ROAD

DRAWING NOT TO SCALE

PARK LANE DEPOT

ALL WIRING ARRANGED IN
A MANNER TO ENABLE
ANTI CLOCKWISE RUNNING
IN THE DEPOT AREA

PERIMETER ROAD

SINGLE VEHICLE PIT

THREE VEHICLE PIT

OFFICES

PARK LANE

DRAWING NOT TO SCALE

Appendix V Fleet List

Standard PSV Circle body codes are used as follows:

Before the seating capacity
B   Single-decker
H   Highbridge double-decker
UH Utility highbridge double-decker

After the seating capacity
C   Centre entrance
R   Rear entrance
D   Dual entrance/exit
RO Rear entrance with outside staircase

Data for each vehicle is given in the following order: fleet number, registration number, chassis number, date into service, date withdrawn (where known; otherwise date delicensed, which may be some time later, indicated thus *)

1	Chassis:	Tilling-Stevens TS6		
	Body:	Dodson B40C		
1	DA 7741	2991	29/10/23	24/03/34 *
2	DA 7742	3034	29/10/23	24/03/34 *
3	DA 7746	3035	29/10/23	24/03/34 *
4	DA 7744	3036	29/10/23	24/03/34 *
5	DA 7745	3037	29/10/23	24/03/34 *
6	DA 7746	3038	29/10/23	24/03/34 *

7	Chassis:	Tilling-Stevens TS6		
	Body:	Dodson B36C		
7	DA 8814	4501	23/08/24	31/10/34 *

8-14	Chassis:	Tilling-Stevens TS6		
	Body:	Dodson B36C		
8	DA 9008	4502	24/01/25	31/08/35 *
9	DA 9009	4504	17/01/25	31/10/35 *
10	DA 9010	4503	28/02/25	31/05/37 *
11	DA 9011	4505	16/03/25	30/06/36 *
12	DA 9012	4507	11/03/25	31/12/35 *
13	DA 9013	4508	10/03/25	31/08/35 *
14	DA 9014	4506	14/03/25	31/12/35 *

15-21	Chassis:	Tilling-Stevens TS6		
	Body:	Dodson B36C		
15	UK 615	4509	26/10/25	31/10/34 *
16	UK 616	4510	26/10/25	31/08/35 *
17	UK 617	4511	27/10/25	01/11/35 *
18	UK 618	4512	26/10/25	30/06/36 *
19	UK 619	4513	27/10/25	31/05/37 *
20	UK 620	4514	29/10/25	31/10/34 *
21	UK 621	4517	09/11/25	31/05/37 *

22-32	Chassis:	Tilling-Stevens TS6		
	Body:	Dodson B36C		
22	UK 622	4515	04/06/27	31/10/34 *
23	UK 623	4516	06/03/26	31/08/35 *
24	UK 624	4522	04/06/27	30/09/34 *
25	UK 625	4518	11/11/26	31/10/34 *
26	UK 626	4519	11/11/26	31/05/37 *
27	UK 627	4521	11/11/26	29/02/36 *
28	UK 628	4525	11/11/26	31/05/37 *
29	UK 629	4520	12/11/26	31/05/37 *
30	UK 630	4524	28/05/27	31/05/37 *
31	UK 631	4523	03/06/27	06/03/36 *
32	UK 632	4526	17/02/26	31/10/34 *

33	Chassis:	Guy BTX		
	Body:	Dodson H33/28RO		
33	UK 633	22131	2/12/26	31/10/36 *

34-40	Chassis:	Guy BTX		
	Body:	Dodson H33/28R		
34	UK 634	22415	08/07/27	28/02/38 *
35	UK 635	22418	11/07/27	28/02/38 *
36	UK 636	22425	15/07/27	28/02/38 *
37	UK 637	22426	11/02/27	28/02/38 *
38	UK 638	22424	10/09/27	30/11/37 *
39	UK 639	22419	17/08/27	30/11/37 *
40	UK 640	22414	19/09/27	30/11/37 *

41-56	Chassis:	Guy BTX		
	Body:	Dodson H33/28R		
41	UK 3941	22416	06/10/27	28/02/38 *
42	UK 3942	22417	24/09/27	30/11/37 *
43	UK 4243	22665	29/11/27	30/11/37 *
44	UK 4244	22664	08/12/27	30/11/37 *
45	UK 4245	22677	01/12/27	28/02/38 *
46	UK 4246	22681	03/12/27	30/09/38 *
47	UK 4247	22676	09/12/27	30/09/38 *
48	UK 4248	22678	16/12/27	30/09/38 *
49	UK 4249	22698	04/01/28	30/09/38 *
50	UK 4250	23078	19/11/28	30/09/38 *
51	UK 5951	23079	19/11/28	30/09/38 *
52	UK 5952	23080	17/11/28	26/08/38 *
53	UK 5953	23077	17/11/28	26/08/38 *
54	UK 5954	23081	19/11/28	30/09/38 *
55	UK 5955	23075	17/11/28	30/09/38 *
56	UK 5956	23076	23/11/28	30/09/38 *

57-61	Chassis:	Guy BTX		
	Body:	Dodson H33/28R		
57	UK 6357	23243	04/05/29	30/09/38 *
58	UK 6358	23246	04/05/29	31/10/40 *
59	UK 6359	23247	27/05/29	31/10/40 *
60	UK 6360	23245	14/05/29	31/10/40 *
61	UK 6361	23244	15/05/29	31/10/40 *

62-70	Chassis:	Guy BTX		
	Body:	Dodson H30/31R		
62	UK 7962	23459	08/01/30	31/12/44 *
63	UK 7963	23460	18/01/30	31/12/44 *
64	UK 7964	23461	25/01/30	01/09/43 *
65	UK 7965	23493	25/01/30	31/12/44 *
66	UK 7966	23446	03/02/30	01/09/43 *
67	UK 8767	23463	21/05/30	01/09/43 *
68	UK 8768	23437	07/06/30	31/12/44 *
69	UK 8769	23464	06/09/30	01/09/43 *
70	UK 8770	23453	20/09/30	31/12/44 *

71-78	Chassis:	Guy BTX		
	Body:	Guy H33/26R		
71	UK 9971	23700	04/04/31	31/07/45 *
72	UK 9972	23701	04/04/31	24/03/45 *
73	UK 9973	23702	03/04/31	31/05/45 *
74	UK 9974	23703	16/05/31	31/05/45 *
75	UK 9975	23706	04/04/31	31/07/45 *
76	UK 9976	23726	18/05/31	31/07/45 *
77	UK 9977	23731	15/05/31	30/06/45 *
78	UK 9978	23732	18/05/31	31/05/45 *

79-82	Chassis:	Guy BTX		
	Body:	Guy H33/26R		
79	JW 579	23768	16/11/31	31/05/45 *
80	JW 580	23769	17/11/31	31/07/45 *
81	JW 581	23770	16/11/31	31/05/45 *
82	JW 582	23771	16/11/31	30/04/46 *

83-91	Chassis:	Guy BTX			
	Body:	Dodson H33/26R			
83	JW 983	23821	01/06/32	28/05/47	*
84	JW 984	23822	01/06/32	31/03/48	*
85	JW 985	23824	01/06/32	28/05/47	*
86	JW 986	23823	07/10/32	28/05/47	*
87	JW 987	23825	07/10/32	28/05/47	*
88	JW 988	23827	07/10/32	28/05/47	*
89	JW 989	23829	31/03/33	28/05/47	*
90	JW 990	23826	31/03/33	28/05/47	*
91	JW 991	23828	01/04/33	31/07/48	*

92-95	Chassis:	Sunbeam MS2			
	Body:	Weymann H31/28R (92-4) or H33/28R (95)			
92	JW 992	12002	01/06/32	31/07/48	*
93	JW 993	12004	01/06/32	31/10/48	*
94	JW 994	12003	02/06/32	31/07/47	*
95	JW 526	12001	08/07/31	31/07/48	*

96-98	Chassis:	Sunbeam MS3			
	Body:	Metro-Cammell H33/25R			
96	JW 3396	12027	16/01/34	31/07/48	*
97	JW 3397	12028	19/01/34	28/05/47	*
98	JW 3398	12029	03/03/34	31/10/46	*

99, 200-203	Chassis:	Guy BTX			
	Body:	Metro-Cammell H33/25R			
99	JW 3399	23963	01/02/34	30/04/46	*
200	JW 3400	23965	03/02/34	31/10/48	*
201	JW 3401	23961	08/02/34	31/08/46	*
202	JW 3402	23962	10/02/34	15/08/47	*
203	JW 3403	23964	17/02/34	31/10/48	*

204, 205	Chassis:	Sunbeam MS3			
	Body:	Metro-Cammell H33/25R			
204	JW 4104	12024	10/01/34	30/09/45	*
205	JW 4105	12025	29/03/34	28/05/47	*

206-209	Chassis:	Sunbeam MF1			
	Body:	Park Royal B32R			
206	JW 4106	13002	30/03/34	24/03/45	*
207	JW 4107	13016	03/12/34	25/03/49	*
208	JW 4108	13017	24/11/34	25/03/49	*
209	JW 4109	13018	15/12/34	25/03/49	*

210-213	Chassis:	Guy BT			
	Body:	Park Royal B32R			
210	JW 4310	24036	03/11/34	31/01/45	*
211	JW 4311	24037	03/11/34	31/01/44	*
212	JW 4312	24038	01/11/34	31/01/45	*
213	JW 4313	24039	01/11/34	31/01/45	*

214-217	Chassis:	Sunbeam MS3			
	Body:	Beadle H33/25R			
214	JW 4314	12043	12/10/34	31/07/48	*
215	JW 4315	12044	01/11/34	23/05/47	*
216	JW 4316	12045	04/12/34	31/07/48	*
217	JW 4317	12046	01/11/34	31/10/48	*

218-221	Chassis:	Guy BTX			
	Body:	Beadle H33/25R			
218	JW 4318	24035	08/10/34	25/03/49	*
219	JW 4319	24034	09/10/34	31/07/48	*
220	JW 4320	24032	01/11/34	25/03/49	*
221	JW 4321	24033	09/01/35	30/04/46	*

222	Chassis:	Sunbeam MS2			
	Body:	Metro-Cammell H31/28R			
222	OC 6567	12008	20/09/34	25/03/49	*

223-226	Chassis:	Sunbeam MS2			
	Body:	Park Royal H33/25R			
223	JW 7323	12145	03/08/35	25/03/49	*
224	JW 7324	12143	03/08/35	25/03/49	*
225	JW 7325	12144	05/08/35	25/03/49	*
226	JW 7326	12146	05/08/35	25/03/49	*

227-230	Chassis:	Guy BTX			
	Body:	Brush H33/25R			
227	JW 7327	24104	20/12/35	01/03/49	*
228	JW 7328	24105	21/12/35	25/03/49	*
229	JW 7329	24107	20/12/35	31/07/48	*
230	JW 7330	24106	26/12/35	25/03/49	*

231-233	Chassis:	Sunbeam MF1			
	Body:	Park Royal B32R			
231	JW 8131	13034	13/01/36	31/01/44	*
232	JW 8132	13052	27/06/36	25/03/49	*
233	JW 8133	13053	27/06/36	25/03/49	*

234-238	Chassis:	Guy BT			
	Body:	Park Royal H28/26R			
234	JW 8134	24183	03/10/36	30/06/49	*
235	JW 8135	24184	15/10/36	30/06/49	*
236	JW 8136	24185	03/10/36	30/06/49	*
237	JW 8137	24186	03/10/36	30/06/49	*
238	JW 8138	24187	03/10/36	30/06/49	*

239-244	Chassis:	Sunbeam MF2			
	Body:	Park Royal H29/26R			
239	JW 8139	13046	18/11/36	31/07/49	*
240	JW 8140	13047	18/11/36	31/07/49	*
241	JW 8141	13048	18/11/36	31/07/49	*
242	JW 8142	13049	21/11/36	31/07/49	*
243	JW 8143	13050	27/03/37	30/06/49	*
244	JW 8144	13051	27/03/37	31/07/49	*

245	Chassis:	Sunbeam MS2			
	Body:	Park Royal H33/25R			
245	JW 8145	12147	26/06/36	25/03/49	*

246-251	Chassis:	Sunbeam MF2			
	Body:	Beadle H28/26R			
246	AJW 46	13055	02/10/37	30/09/49	*
247	AJW 47	13056	02/10/37	31/08/49	*
248	AJW 48	13057	13/10/37	30/09/49	*
249	AJW 49	13058	22/10/37	31/07/49	*
250	AJW 50	13059	23/11/37	31/08/49	*
251	AJW 51	13060	01/12/37	30/09/49	*

252-258	Chassis:	Guy BT			
	Body:	Beadle H28/26R			
252	AJW 52	22452	19/11/37	31/10/49	*
253	AJW 53	22453	20/11/37	31/07/49	*
254	AJW 54	22454	27/11/37	31/10/49	*
255	AJW 55	22455	01/12/37	31/10/49	*
256	AJW 56	22611	10/12/37	30/06/49	*
257	AJW 57	22457	04/12/37	30/06/49	*
258	BDA 358	22456	18/12/37	30/09/49	*

259-263	Chassis:	Guy BT			
	Body:	Roe H29/25R			
259	BDA 359	24612	05/02/38	30/09/49	*
260	BDA 360	24613	12/02/38	30/09/49	*
261	BDA 361	24614	12/02/38	31/08/49	*
262	BDA 362	24615	05/02/38	31/01/50	*
263	BDA 363	24616	12/02/38	30/11/49	*

264-275	Chassis:	Sunbeam MF2			
	Body:	Park Royal H28/26R			
264	BDA 364	13069	24/12/37	30/11/49	*
265	BDA 365	13070	10/03/38	30/11/49	*
266	BDA 366	13071	19/03/38	31/01/50	*
267	BDA 367	13072	02/04/38	30/11/49	*
268	BDA 368	13073	09/04/38	30/11/49	*
269	BDA 369	13074	16/04/38	31/01/50	*
270	BJW 170	13075	01/08/38	21/11/49	*
271	BJW 171	13076	01/08/38	31/01/50	*
272	BJW 172	13077	23/08/38	31/10/49	*
273	BJW 173	13078	06/09/38	31/01/50	*
274	BJW 174	13079	24/08/38	20/10/49	*
275	BJW 175	13080	14/09/38	31/01/50	*

276-281	Chassis:	Guy BT			
	Body:	Roe H29/25R			
276	BJW 176	24676	20/08/38	31/10/49	*
277	BJW 177	24677	27/08/38	30/09/53	*
278	BJW 178	24678	27/08/38	22/04/50	*
279	BJW 179	24679	08/09/38	30/11/49	*
280	BJW 180	24680	15/09/38	30/06/53	*
281	BJW 181	24681	17/09/38	30/11/49	*

282-285	Chassis:	Sunbeam MF2			
	Body:	Park Royal H28/26R (282/3)			
		or Roe H29/25R (284/5)			
282	DDA 182	13081	20/03/40	24/03/52	*
283	DDA 183	13107	20/07/40	30/11/50	*
284	DDA 184	13109	10/06/40	30/11/50	*
285	DDA 185	13108	21/06/40	30/11/50	*

286-295	Chassis:	Sunbeam MF2			
	Body:	Park Royal H28/26R (286-90)			
		or Roe H29/25R (291-5)			
286	DDA 986	13111	04/03/42	29/02/52	*
287	DDA 987	13112	13/03/42	24/03/52	*
288	DDA 988	13113	18/02/42	29/02/52	*
289	DDA 989	13114	21/02/42	24/03/52	*
290	DDA 990	13115	27/10/42	29/02/52	*
291	DDA 991	13116	07/02/42	29/02/52	*
292	DDA 992	13117	06/02/42	29/02/52	*
293	DDA 993	13118	19/02/42	24/03/52	*
294	DDA 994	13119	12/02/42	29/02/52	*
295	DDA 995	13120	04/04/42	24/03/52	*

296-299, 400, 401	Chassis:	Sunbeam W4			
	Body:	Weymann UH30/26R			
296	DJW 596	50023	03/07/43	30/09/53	*
297	DJW 597	50024	08/07/43	30/09/53	*
298	DJW 598	50025	17/07/43	30/09/53	*
299	DJW 599	50026	28/08/43	30/09/53	*
400	DJW 600	50027	04/08/43	30/09/53	*
401	DJW 601	50028	13/08/43	30/09/53	*

402-407	Chassis:	Sunbeam W4			
	Body:	Park Royal UH30/26R			
		(see also table of rebodied vehicles)			
402	DJW 902	50095	16/12/44	09/06/63	
403	DJW 903	50096	05/12/44	08/10/65	*
404	DJW 904	50097	01/12/44	09/06/63	
405	DJW 905	50098	30/11/44	03/02/64	*
406	DJW 906	50099	11/11/44	31/07/65	*
407	DJW 907	50100	16/11/44	26/01/64	*

408-418	Chassis:	Sunbeam W4			
	Body:	Weymann UH30/26R (408) or Park Royal UH30/26R (remainder)			
		(see also table of rebodied vehicles)			
408	DJW 938	50141	07/05/45	31/10/65	
409	DJW 939	50142	05/05/45	31/10/65	
410	DJW 940	50143	05/05/45	31/07/65	*
411	DJW 941	50144	05/05/45	31/10/65	
412	DJW 942	50145	05/05/45	03/11/63	
413	DJW 943	50146	17/05 45	31/10/65	
414	DUK 14	50151	06/07/45	03/11/63	
415	DUK 15	50152	11/11/45	08/08/65	
416	DUK 16	50153	21/07/45	08/08/65	
417	DUK 17	50154	02/07/45	31/07/65	*
418	DUK 18	50155	21/07/45	31/10/65	

419-433	Chassis:	Sunbeam W4			
	Body:	Park Royal UH30/26R			
		(see also table of rebodied vehicles)			
419	DUK 419	50297	25/03/46	26/12/63	
420	DUK 820	50298	25/03/46	31/10/65	
421	DUK 821	50299	25/11/46	31/10/65	
422	DUK 822	50300	25/03/46	31/10/65	
423	DUK 823	50301	01/04/46	31/10/65	
424	DUK 824	50302	30/04/46	06/03/67	*
425	DUK 825	50303	01/04/46	06/03/67	*
426	DUK 826	50304	22/05/46	06/03/67	*
427	DUK 827	50306	22/05/46	06/03/67	*
428	DUK 828	50305	22/06/46	31/10/65	*
429	DUK 829	50307	05/06/46	06/03/67	*
430	DUK 830	50308	05/06/46	17/01/66	*
431	DUK 831	50309	12/06/46	11/07/66	
432	DUK 832	50310	07/06/46	06/03/67	*
433	DUK 833	50311	05/06/46	06/03/67	*

434-455	Chassis:	Sunbeam W4			
	Body:	Park Royal H28/26R			
		(see also table of rebodied vehicles)			
434	EJW 434	50365	08/05/47	05/01/67	
435	EJW 435	50366	09/04/47	06/03/67	*
436	EJW 436	50367	04/05/47	22/11/66	*
437	EJW 437	50368	15/04/47	06/03/67	*
438	EJW 438	50369	25/04/47	06/03/67	*
439	EJW 439	50370	03/04/47	06/03/67	*
440	EJW 440	50371	05/04/47	06/03/67	*
441	EJW 441	50372	06/04/47	24/02/67	*
442	EJW 442	50373	10/05/47	05/01/67	
443	EJW 443	50374	28/03/47	06/03/67	*
444	EJW 444	50375	12/12/47	05/03/67	
445	EJW 445	50376	11/12/47	18/01/65	
446	EJW 446	50377	17/12/47	05/03/67	
447	EJW 447	50378	23/12/47	05/03/67	
448	EJW 448	50379	19/12/47	05/03/67	
449	EJW 449	50380	01/01/48	05/03/67	
450	EJW 450	50381	03/01/48	26/01/64	
451	EJW 451	50382	26/01/48	05/03/67	
452	EJW 452	50383	15/01/48	05/03/67	
453	EJW 453	50384	17/01/48	06/03/67	*
454	EJW 454	50385	17/01/48	05/03/67	
455	EJW 455	50386	24/01/48	05/03/67	

456-481	Chassis:	Sunbeam F4		
	Body:	Park Royal H28/26R		
456	FJW 456	50521	03/09/48	09/06/63
457	FJW 457	50522	03/09/48	08/08/65
458	FJW 458	50523	04/09/48	31/12/61
459	FJW 459	50524	11/09/48	28/02/61 *
460	FJW 460	50525	04/09/48	09/06/63
461	FJW 461	50526	11/09/48	09/08/65
462	FJW 462	50527	18/09/48	26/01/64 *
463	FJW 463	50528	18/09/48	09/06/63
464	FJW 464	50529	14/10/48	25/11/64 *
465	FJW 465	50530	09/10/48	08/08/65
466	FJW 466	50531	20/10/48	31/07/65 *
467	FJW 467	50532	02/10/48	09/06/63
468	FJW 468	50533	16/10/48	08/08/65
469	FJW 469	50534	23/10/48	09/06/63
470	FJW 470	50535	23/10/48	09/06/63
471	FJW 471	50536	18/09/48	25/11/64
472	FJW 472	50537	09/10/48	03/11/63
473	FJW 473	50538	09/10/48	08/08/65
474	FJW 474	50539	18/09/48	26/01/64
475	FJW 475	50540	16/10/48	26/01/64 *
476	FJW 476	50541	25/09/48	25/10/64
477	FJW 477	50542	30/10/48	26/01/64 *
478	FJW 478	50543	30/10/48	25/10/65
479	FJW 479	50544	06/11/48	25/10/64
480	FJW 480	50545	05/10/48	09/06/63
481	FJW 481	50546	06/11/48	09/06/63

482-499,	Chassis:	Guy BT		
600-607	Body:	Park Royal H28/26R		
482	FJW 482	36974	18/06/49	09/06/63
483	FJW 483	36975	16/04/49	09/06/63
484	FJW 484	36976	16/04/49	25/10/64
485	FJW 485	36977	16/04/49	16/11/61 *
486	FJW 486	36978	16/04/49	09/06/63
487	FJW 487	36979	04/06/49	03/11/63
488	FJW 488	36980	17/06/49	03/11/63
489	FJW 489	36981	04/06/49	03/11/63
490	FJW 490	36982	25/06/49	04/11/63
491	FJW 491	36983	25/06/49	09/06/63
492	FJW 492	36984	04/06/49	29/09/63
493	FJW 493	36985	17/06/49	26/01/64 *
494	FJW 494	36986	04/06/49	29/09/63
495	FJW 495	36987	18/06/49	29/09/63
496	FJW 496	36988	10/09/49	26/01/64 *
497	FJW 497	36989	17/09/49	29/09/63
498	FJW 498	36990	03/09/49	08/08/65
499	FJW 499	36991	10/09/49	26/01/64 *
600	FJW 600	36992	10/09/49	03/11/63
601	FJW 601	36993	03/09/49	26/01/64
602	FJW 602	36994	28/09/49	11/09/62 *
603	FJW 603	36995	01/10/49	26/01/64 *
604	FJW 604	36996	01/10/49	26/01/64 *
605	FJW 605	36997	01/10/49	26/01/64 *
606	FJW 606	36998	01/10/49	26/01/64 *
607	FJW 607	36999	01/10/49	26/01/64 *

608-630	Chassis:	Sunbeam F4		
	Body:	Park Royal H28/26R		
608	FJW 608	50639	03/03/49	03/11/63
609	FJW 609	50640	03/03/49	28/02/62 *
610	FJW 610	50641	07/03/49	03/11/63
611	FJW 611	50642	03/03/49	03/11/63
612	FJW 612	50643	05/03/49	03/11/63
613	FJW 613	50644	05/03/49	03/11/63
614	FJW 614	50645	17/03/49	03/11/63
615	FJW 615	50646	10/03/49	09/09/63
616	FJW 616	50647	12/03/49	03/11/63
617	FJW 617	50648	16/03/49	31/08/63 *
618	FJW 618	50649	14/03/49	29/09/63
619	FJW 619	50650	17/03/49	03/11/63
620	FJW 620	50651	25/03/49	03/11/63
621	FJW 621	50652	04/04/49	26/01/64 *
622	FJW 622	50653	26/03/49	03/11/63
623	FJW 623	50712	25/03/50	31/01/62 *
624	FJW 624	50713	25/03/50	09/06/63
625	FJW 625	50714	29/03/50	08/08/65
626	FJW 626	50715	04/04/50	08/08/65
627	FJW 627	50716	02/05/50	26/01/64 *
628	FJW 628	50717	02/05/50	28/02/62 *
629	FJW 629	50718	02/05/50	28/02/62 *
630	FJW 630	50719	02/05/50	25/10/64

631-654	Chassis:	Guy BT		
	Body:	Park Royal H28/26R		
631	FJW 631	37000	03/11/49	03/11/63
632	FJW 632	37001	04/11/49	08/08/65
633	FJW 633	37002	07/11/49	26/01/64 *
634	FJW 634	37003	01/12/49	26/01/64 *
635	FJW 635	37004	09/11/49	26/01/64 *
636	FJW 636	37005	12/11/49	26/01/64 *
637	FJW 637	37006	12/11/49	03/11/63
638	FJW 638	37007	01/12/49	03/11/63
639	FJW 639	37008	01/12/49	03/11/63
640	FJW 640	37009	01/12/49	03/11/63
641	FJW 641	37010	01/12/49	03/11/63 *
642	FJW 642	37012	08/12/49	03/11/63
643	FJW 643	37014	17/12/49	03/11/63
644	FJW 644	37011	17/12/49	26/01/64 *
645	FJW 645	37013	03/01/50	23/06/63
646	FJW 646	37015	04/01/50	08/08/65
647	FJW 647	37016	14/01/50	28/02/61 *
648	FJW 648	37017	01/03/50	15/11/62 *
649	FJW 649	37018	02/03/50	26/01/64 *
650	FJW 650	37019	30/03/50	25/10/64
651	FJW 651	37020	06/03/50	08/07/64
652	FJW 652	37021	22/04/50	08/08/65
653	FJW 653	37022	08/04/50	28/02/62 *
654	FJW 654	37023	08/04/50	08/08/65

Notes

Low-voltage (12V) lighting was fitted to trolleybuses 96-99 and 200-245. All others had lighting from the traction supply, with lamps in series at 50V or 130V.

Wartime deliveries of trolleybuses were initially painted grey; so treated were Nos 290/6-9 and 400-18. Additionally, trolleybuses 402-7 were fitted with wooden seats as a wartime economy measure.

Standard livery was apple green on the lower panels with primrose-yellow upper panels. In the period 1930-40 a number of trolleys initially carried a mainly green livery, these being Nos 65, 74/7/9, 80/5/6/8, 95-8, 200-5/15/8-22/7-30/54-63/5-82, Nos 254-63/5-82 being delivered in this livery and the others being repainted subsequently. No 290 was delivered in wartime grey. One odd man out was 99, on which cream was used in lieu of primrose. The 1959 trials involved six trolleys — 409, 412, 471, 490, 603.and 653 — which carried a livery of all-over dark green, relieved by a single straw-coloured waistband. All were eventually repainted in the standard livery with the exception of 653, which retained the dark-green colour until withdrawal.

Rebodied trolleybuses

Fleet No	Into service (first body)	Into service (second body)	Fleet No	Into service (first body)	Into service (second body)
402	16/12/44 Park Royal UH30/26R	14/02/52 Park Royal H28/26R	429	05/06/46 Park Royal UH30/26R	29/10/58 Roe H32/28R
403	05/12/44 Park Royal UH30/26R	01/03/52 Park Royal H28/26R	430	05/06/46 Park Royal UH30/26R	07/09/59 Roe H32/28R
404	01/12/44 Park Royal UH30/26R	03/03/52 Park Royal H28/26R	431	12/06/46 Park Royal UH30/26R	18/11/58 Roe H32/28R
405	30/11/44 Park Royal UH30/26R	11/03/52 Park Royal H28/26R	432	07/06/46 Park Royal UH30/26R	06/10/59 Roe H32/28R
406	11/11/44 Park Royal UH30/26R	08/03/52 Park Royal H28/26R	433	05/06 46 Park Royal UH30/26R	14/09/59 Roe H32/28R
407	16/11/44 Park Royal UH30/26R	22/03/52 Park Royal H28/26R	434	06/05/47 Park Royal H28/26R	25/03/60 Roe H32/28R
408	17/05/45 Weymann UH30/26R	25/03/52 Park Royal H28/26R	435	17/04/47 Park Royal H28/26R	01/01/62 Roe H32/28R
409	05/05/45 Park Royal UH30/26R	31/03/52 Park Royal H28/26R	436	02/05 47 Park Royal H28/26R	12/01/62 Roe H32/28R
410	05/05/45 Park Royal UH30/26R	25/04/52 Park Royal H28/26R	437	14/04/47 Park Royal H28/26R	01/02/62 Roe H32/28R
411	05/05/45 Park Royal UH30/26R	01/04/52 Park Royal H28/26R	438	24/04/47 Park Royal H28/26R	11/05/60 Roe H32/28R
412	05/05/45 Park Royal UH30/26R	18/03/52 Park Royal H28/26R	439	01/04/47 Park Royal H28/26R	11/01/60 Roe H32/28R
413	17/05/45 Park Royal UH30/26R	07/05/52 Park Royal H28/26R	440	02/04/47 Park Royal H28/26R	20/02/61 Roe H32/28R
414	06/07/45 Park Royal UH30/26R	16/03/52 Park Royal H28/26R	441	25/04/47 Park Royal H28/26R	18/06/60 Roe H32/28R
415	18/11/45 Park Royal UH30/26R	31/03/52 Park Royal H28/26R	442	09/05/47 Park Royal H28/26R	11/08/60 Roe H32/28R
416	21/07/45 Park Royal UH30/26R	07/05/52 Park Royal H28/26R	443	14/03/47 Park Royal H28/26R	07/02/62 Roe H32/28R
417	02/07/45 Park Royal UH30/26R	07/05/52 Park Royal H28/26R	444	17/12/47 Park Royal H28/26R	11/08/60 Roe H32/28R
418	21/07/45 Park Royal UH30/26R	24/06/59 Roe H32/28R	445	09/12/47 Park Royal H28/26R	14/02/62 Roe H32/28R
419	18/03/46 Park Royal UH30/26R	18/11/58 Roe H32/28R	446	16/12/47 Park Royal H28/26R	19/01/62 Roe H32/28R
420	18/03/46 Park Royal UH30/26R	29/12/58 Roe H32/28R	447	22/12/47 Park Royal H28/26R	18/04/61 Roe H32/28R
421	20/11/46 Park Royal UH30/26R	14/08/58 Roe H32/28R	448	18/12/47 Park Royal H28/26R	02/02/61 Roe H32/28R
422	21/03/46 Park Royal UH30/26R	04/09/58 Roe H32/28R	449	24/12/47 Park Royal H28/26R	26/04/61 Roe H32/28R
423	25/03/46 Park Royal UH30/26R	14/05/59 Roe H32/28R	450	29/12/47 Park Royal H28/26R	01/02/62 Roe H32/28R
424	27/03/46 Park Royal UH30/26R	13/06/59 Roe H32/28R	451	22/01/48 Park Royal H28/26R	11/04/61 Roe H32/28R
425	29/03/46 Park Royal UH30/26R	01/05/59 Roe H32/28R	452	12/01/48 Park Royal H28/26R	14/09/60 Roe H32/28R
426	22/04/46 Park Royal UH30/26R	06/08 58 Roe H32/28R	453	14/01/48 Park Royal H28/26R	04/10/60 Roe H32/28R
427	22/04/46 Park Royal UH30/26R	03/07/59 Roe H32/28R	454	14/01/48 Park Royal H28/26R	05/04/60 Roe H32/28R
428	22/06/46 Park Royal UH30/26R	23/09/58 Roe H32/28R	455	22/01/48 Park Royal H28/26R	01/03/61 Roe H32/28R

Above: A Corporation photograph, taken at Park Lane depot, of Sunbeam W4 trolley 412 after rebodying in 1952. *John Hughes collection*

Service Vehicles

Over the years many specialist ancillary vehicles have been needed to deal with the day-to-day maintenance and support of the trolleybus system. Conversion of withdrawn buses created some of the early examples.

Tower wagons

No	Registration	Chassis	In service	Notes
	DA 1350	Albion	1920-8	Formerly bus 3
	DA 2781	Tilling-Stevens	1928/9	Formerly bus 7
1	DA 3623	Tilling-Stevens	1928-32	Formerly bus 9
	DA 3622	Tilling-Stevens	1928-32	Formerly bus 10
	DA 3624	Tilling-Stevens	1928-32	Formerly bus 11
2	DA 9031	Tilling-Stevens	1932-47	Formerly bus 31; tower from DA 3622
1	DA 9032	Tilling-Stevens	1933-47	Formerly bus 32; tower from DA 3623
3	DA 9033	Tilling-Stevens	1932-47	Formerly bus 33; tower from DA 3624
	UX 1181	Sunbeam	1932-43	Touring-car chassis with light tower
4	DDA 882	Ford Thames	1942-59	Tower built by Eagle, Warwick
5	EOP 505	Humber Hawk	1943-55	Fitted with light-duty tower from UX 1181
6	JW 5792	Daimler COG5	1945-61	Formerly bus 192
7	EUK 770	Guy Vixen	1947-67	Tower by Eagle, Warwick
8	EUK 771	Guy Vixen	1947-64	Tower by Eagle, Warwick
1	WDA 301	Guy Warrior	1958-67	Tower by Robinson, Wolverhampton
2	WDA 302	Guy Warrior	1959-71	Tower by Robinson, Wolverhampton

Other vehicles

Registration	Chassis	In service	Notes
JW 5793	Daimler COG5	1948-61	Poling wagon; formerly bus 193
6384 JW	Austin 7-ton	1961-6	Poling wagon
LJW 348D	Ford D750	1966-9	Dropside poling wagon
DA 3625	Tilling-Stevens	1928-47	Tipping wagon; formerly bus 12
EJW 955	Guy Vixen	1947-60	Tipping lorry
2024 JW	Thames Trader	1960-9	Tipping lorry
053 UK *	Canadian Ford	1946-67	Towing wagon; ex WD
013 DA *	AEC Matador III	1962-9	Towing wagon; ex RAF
FJW 561	Guy Arab III	1963-71	Snowplough; ex bus 561
FJW 563	Guy Arab III	1963-71	Snowplough; ex bus 563

* trade plates

Appendix VI Survivors

With the final closure, efforts were made to preserve a number of trolleybuses in different locations, but sadly these did not all come to fruition. The '402' class of Sunbeam W4 utility trolleys are a good example of this; 408 was an excellent runner, admired by staff and enthusiasts alike, becoming something of a pet after the 1964 tour. They are much missed, especially as examples of both the Sunbeam F4 and Guy BT 8ft-wide trolleys have survived (albeit in poor condition), as has 433, the Roe-bodied Sunbeam W4. It is to be regretted that no serious effort was mounted to save a utility for preservation, thus completing the trio of body styles to be seen in the closing years of the system.

432

Initially stored at Bilston depot in 1967 for eventual display of the chassis at Birmingham Science Museum, but the plan was withdrawn. Became donor of parts for restoration of 433. Sold in November 1970 and scrapped in 1971.

446

This trolley had the distinction of working the last service journey under wires from Dudley to Wolverhampton at 11.12pm on Sunday 5 March 1967 and as such was an ideal candidate for preservation. After arrival at Cleveland Road it was towed straight to Bilston depot for potential preservation, but it too was scrapped, in September 1968. The movements to Bilston could explain rumours (which persisted for many weeks after closure) of a strategic reserve of trolleybuses held somewhere on the system.

449

Sold to Don Everall in 1967 and purchased by the Trolleybus Group. Subsequently dismantled for spare parts to use in the restoration of 433.

467

Sold in 1963 to Don Everall and survived in use as a caravan until 1972. The NTA obtained a number of parts for use on two other trolleys in its care, 616 and 654.

Fortunately four trolleybuses are known to have survived closure.

78

Having been sold out of service on 30 August 1945 to Don Everall, the afterlife of this hardy survivor is somewhat of a mystery. It was re-discovered by the Tramway Museum Society of Ireland, lying in a field at Callan, near Kilkenny in the Republic of Ireland. It was rescued and brought back to the Black Country Living Museum in Dudley in June 1990 and is now under the care of the Black Country Museum Transport Group. Much of the running gear and chassis is complete, though the nearside body had suffered severe rot. It is in a poor/semi dismantled state and awaiting restoration.

433

This was also stored at Bilston depot after closure, for display at the Science Museum. Restoration was done by the Wolverhampton Trolleybus Group with assistance from the

West Midlands Passenger Transport Executive (successors to the Transport Department in October 1969). The Science Museum withdrew its proposal for the display and it was moved to the Black Country Living Museum. It is in flagship condition and presently operating on the museum route system.

616

This was presented to the Railway Preservation Society in 1964 and initially stored at Hednesford. Subsequently acquired by the NTA and then the Birmingham & Midland Motor Omnibus Trust, it had several homes, most recently having been moved from the St Helens Transport Museum, which had to be emptied for the roof to be replaced and is now in store at the Wythall premises of BaMMOT. It is in a poor and uncared for condition overall and awaits static restoration.

654

This passed to the National Trolleybus Association upon closure of the system. It has received little treatment over the years and is now in a near-derelict condition and in semi open storage at Roade, near Northampton. However, as a result of intransigence on the part of certain individuals within the association, sadly, this trolleybus now faces a bleak and uncertain future with no sign of any restoration work taking place.

Today preserved trolleybuses can be viewed at many static exhibits around the country. There are also three active working sites, which are well worth a visit. The Trolleybus Museum at Sandtoft, to the west of Scunthorpe, Lincolnshire, and the East Anglia Transport

Museum at Carlton Colville, near Lowestoft, Suffolk, both have short sections of wiring for operating trolleybuses, the former having erected many different items of overhead pointwork etc, whilst the latter is able to field operation of motor buses, trams and trolleybuses contemporaneously on the same site. The jewel in the crown, however, must surely be the Black Country Museum Transport Group, located within the Black Country Living Museum in Dudley, Worcestershire. Here can be found the world's only operational double-deck trolleybus route, which now runs extensively through the museum site. At the height of the season up to four of the museum's trolleybuses operate on a 10-minute headway. Special weekend events are also laid on, with many visiting trolleybuses running alongside the museum's own fleet, in perfect harmony with their surroundings. The Transport Group has an enviable reputation for quality restoration, having tackled much 'no hope' work for other centres, turning derelict rusting hulks into operational, pristine trolleybuses, fully up to the standard of their original finish. A trip to the museum will re-kindle bygone memories and transport the visitor back in time, surrounded by traction poles, overhead wiring and most importantly, lots of working trolleybuses, with their distinctive, yet quiet sound. Familiar sights such as the red-painted compulsory stop signs adorn the streets and the large three-sided clock from Victoria Square hangs again at the top of a traction pole, for all to see. Once more it is possible to re-live those happier days in the past, when, standing on a street corner outside the local shop and anticipating the trip to town, you could always 'Catch the Trolley'.

Above: The Black Country Living Museum Transport Group's flagship preserved trolleybus, Wolverhampton 433, a Sunbeam W4 with bodywork by Charles Roe, being put through its paces at a gala event in 2002. The quality of restoration is a tribute to all involved and a joy to behold. Note the Victoria Square clock, also preserved for posterity. *Author*

Left: No 433 approaches the tramway crossing on the museum's own trolleybus circuit — the world's only fully operational double-deck route. The trolleybus depot can be seen in the background at the top of the hill, with other trolleybuses clustered outside. *Author*

Right: Heading towards the 'town' terminus, 433 will shortly pass Broad Street canal bridge, once the haunt of trolleys on routes 6 and 59 and also preserved for posterity but sadly not currently accessible to trolleys at the museum. *Author*

Left: At the town terminus 433 stands once more in the company of a Walsall Corporation trolleybus, in this instance 862, a Sunbeam F4A with Willowbrook bodywork — proof, if ever it were needed, that the spirit of the trolleybus did not die on that fateful day in March 1967. *Author*